March 1953

To,

Dear Mrs Tawney

With all good wishes & sincere thanks for her interest & appreciation -

Florence Rutter

CHILD ARTISTS OF THE AUSTRALIAN BUSH

CHILD ARTISTS OF THE AUSTRALIAN BUSH

by

MARY DURACK MILLER

in association with

FLORENCE RUTTER

Fully illustrated in colour and monochrome

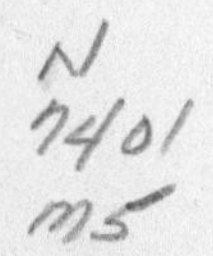

GEORGE G. HARRAP & CO. LTD
LONDON TORONTO WELLINGTON SYDNEY

First published 1952
by George G. Harrap & Co. Ltd
182 High Holborn, London, W.C.1

Dewey Decimal classification: 572.994

Composed in Garamond type and printed by
Western Printing Services Ltd, Bristol

Made in Great Britain

men such as these are not freaks of their kind, though, for members of their race, most of them had unusual opportunities.

The Australian native has never appeared to battle much on his own behalf, but on the whole he has exercised a passive, probably unconscious, resistance to the white man's efforts both for and against him. The white community may formulate slogans—'Assimilation by Organized Breeding' or 'Assimilation, but No Miscegenation'—but the aboriginal will not be organized into assimilation, nor, when he has attained educational and industrial equality with the white, will any slogan prevent the natural process of miscegenation.

Already in New South Wales, Victoria, and the Northern Territory all people of mixed blood not living on native reserves have, in principle, the status of white citizens. Throughout Australia full-blood as well as mixed-blood aborigines may now apply for exemption from the jurisdiction of Native Affairs Departments and for full citizenship, but outside the Northern Territory the birthright of citizenship at the age of twenty-one is still withheld. A man without a vote, the aboriginal has never represented a popular cause, and his needs remain not *rights* so much as matters for the attention of charity. So far we have found no substitute measure for equipping a people for citizenship to declaring them citizens, and this, in the case of the aboriginal, we hesitate to do lest he should abuse such freedoms as represent to him the most attractive aspects of a living-pattern learned from the white.

Although it may be said that no immediate happiness lay for the black man in denying his sacred past, that civilization has starved and beggared him as his life as a simple, nomad hunter never did in former days, these are facts to which the forces of nature are supremely indifferent. We cannot thrust back into the wilderness those who have already emerged, nor keep there those who still hesitate between the dubious advantages of the white man's way of life and the now equally dubious joys of the savage. The future of the aboriginal lies in assimilation into our society and in the opportunity to regain, in a different way, the happiness, well-being, and sense of *belonging to the land* that were lost to him after the coming of the white man. His past and his future are parts of a process that we can retard or hasten, but cannot *stop*.

The character of the coloured people differs to a great extent according to history and environment. In the south of Western

PREFACE

This story of a group of child artists whose extraordinary work flourished for a few years on a Government native settlement in the Great Southern District of Western Australia carries wide implications. It embraces the problem of institutional children, of misfits and unwanteds, the world over, and throws sidelights on general educational problems not confined to the teaching of coloured children. The account of how their art-work developed, touching as it does on the vexed question of the extent to which art should be *taught* or *influenced*, must interest all engaged in the education of the young. The inference would seem to be, not so much that these fifty-odd native children were individually and uniquely gifted, as that most children, given the right encouragement and incentive, *can draw*. However, only the child with the rarest talent is likely to pursue an artistic career, and what remains to be determined is how this natural facility, when once established, can best be used in the child's general development. The tragedy of the native child artists of this story is that their success led only into blind alleys.

Explanations of the development of a group of juvenile artists in so unlikely a place as the Carrolup Native Settlement must be left to experts in the field of education and psychology. The object of this book is no more than to put forward certain facts in the hope that they may become stepping-stones to an understanding of a complicated problem and a lost and lovable people.

Conditions are improving for the coloured people of Australia, but progress is still slow and faltering. When the whole story is told it will be seen that the natives, so long inarticulate, are contributing largely to their own advancement. The things they have been unable to say in words they are saying with increasing volume in art, music, sport, and on the battlefield. Albert Namatjira and his fellow-artists of Central Australia; the tenor Harold Blair; Reg Saunders, captain of a company in Korea; those like Ron Richards and Doug Nicholls, whose names number among our finest athletes, all those who donned the uniform of the Australian soldier to fight for a way of life that was denied them—

Australia we find a more hopeless dependence and degeneracy than in the north, where the coloured man far outnumbers the white and is realizing that his are virtually *the people of the country*, adapted to climatic conditions intolerable to the majority of whites. In the outback districts particularly we have half- and quarter-caste people who are accepted entirely on their merits as good workers and who are already well enough adapted to present-day conditions. These facts need to be stated because of the tendency to dismiss an entire people as intrinsically hopeless. Prejudice inevitably retards progress, and it is difficult in districts where labour was once cheap and reasonably willing to smile upon a generation demanding education and rights that not only greatly inconvenience the white man, but would seem also in their earliest manifestations to bewilder and unstabilize the native.

A rough census shows that there are in Australia to-day about 77,000 people classified as aborigines. Of these about 30,000 are part white. Some 28,000 of the total are in Western Australia. The mixed-coloured population is increasing fairly rapidly, and there are indications that the decline in the full-blood population is being halted, and that soon there may be an increase.

In many respects native administration faces knottier problems to-day than ever before. It has come to the cross-roads where the old order of protection must be replaced by one of progressive social advancement. The Department of Native Affairs has always striven for what it currently saw as the best policy for the people in its care. It is in the unfortunate position of being regarded with suspicion by the natives, as interfering with their individual freedoms, and with dislike by the white population, in whose eyes it can do no right. Successive Commissioners have sought to right the wrongs of the past. They have exhausted themselves in fighting the Government for funds, coping with staff troubles, endeavouring to gain the confidence of the natives and the co-operation of the whites. Policy has always necessarily been experimental and subject to a constant process of trial and error.

In Western Australia a broadening Departmental policy gives confidence for the future of such children as the young artists with whose story we are here principally concerned. It will be seen that there was no lack of good intentions on their behalf, that every one concerned wished nothing but the advancement of the children, but that frustration arose through the conflict of ideas as to how their welfare should best be served.

My thanks are due to our present Commissioner of Native Affairs, Mr S. G. Middleton, who made possible my visit to the Carrolup Native Settlement before its reconstruction as a technical training centre, and also to other native institutions in the Great Southern District. Mr Middleton has been most helpful in making available all necessary material and in putting before me a clear and honest picture of Departmental difficulties and plans.

My thanks are due also to Inspector C. S. Crabbe and Mr. J. P. Stokes, of the Educational Department, for presenting the educational side of the Carrolup story, and to Mr and Mrs Noel White, an account of whose brave and selfless efforts on behalf of the child artists is given in this book, and who helped with much information regarding their native pupils.

To Mrs Florence Rutter I am most indebted for having urged the writing and collaborated in the preparation of this book, the production of which is due so largely to her enthusiasm and faith and to her capacity for inspiring these qualities in others. Where many had lost heart in the complications involved she has remained steadfast to a promise made to a group of barefooted waifs in the heart of the Australian bush—that she would endeavour, by every means in her power, to make their work known through the world and thereby assist them and their people to citizenship.

MARY DURACK MILLER

PERTH
WESTERN AUSTRALIA

CONTENTS

ILLUSTRATIONS

The following reproductions of the child artists' work are arranged in a separate section at the end of the book. Details of the paintings are given at page 79.

CHAPTER ONE

CHILDREN OF CARROLUP

THE visitor stood entranced before this array of pictures on the schoolroom walls. Painted on odd scraps of paper, the landscapes glowed with colour and life. Here was none of the approved crudity and distortion of accepted 'child art.' Here was a precision of drawing and perspective, a boldness and harmony of design and colour, sometimes an almost Oriental delicacy and economy of line, though the work was not an adaptation of any known art-form. In style it was unique, un-self-conscious, but showing a surprising confidence, almost a sophistication. It was, the visitor believed, an exhibition of skill not to be equalled by children anywhere in the world. She pointed to a large pastel in soft greys—a landscape portraying bounding kangaroos among gum-trees.

"Whose work is this?"

A boy of about thirteen, prodded and nudged by his companions, shyly admitted ownership, and was urged to point out other examples of his work—"Dawn," "Kangaroo contemplating," "Big Tree."

"Your work is very beautiful. What do you want to be when you grow up?"

The boy shuffled in embarrassment.

"I want to be something *good*."

"What kind of thing?"

"Aw—baking bread, or printing, might be—or driving a truck."

"You could be a great artist. You'd like that, wouldn't you?"

The boy's puckish face lit up with merriment.

"All the children here can draw."

The visitor agreed that it was difficult to single out any child's work as superior to the rest, nor was she able to discover which one had established the characteristic style in which most of the pictures were executed.

The teacher explained that his pupils had been left entirely to their own tastes and inclinations. The girls had delighted in working out imaginative and subtle designs, suitable, perhaps, for dress materials or furnishing fabrics, while the boys' work was bolder, more definite and literal, portraying landscapes, animals, and hunting-scenes. He had not taught the children to draw, though he had stimulated and encouraged them.

"And what of their future?" the visitor asked when the class had been dismissed.

Mr Noel White, a tall, slight man, spread expressive hands.

"I am told they have no future."

"But they are quite remarkable. Their country should be proud of them."

The teacher's dark eyes, quick to light with fun and laughter, were deeply sad.

"They have no country."

The visitor was puzzled.

"Where, then, were they born?"

"Some here at Carrolup, some in the bush, some in hovels on the rubbish-tips of country towns."

"But they have talent, and their faces are bright with intelligence. Surely they hope for better things?"

"I think they do most earnestly, but the situation is very involved. All over Australia there are groups of children like these. It is hard to know how to explain or where to start."

The visitor smiled.

"Then let us keep to the few simple facts we have here. There are no doubt many in need of help, but I am not young. I cannot hope to help a whole people, but this little group here—surely there is something I could do."

The problem seemed straightforward enough to one accustomed to organizing, anxious to assist so clear a cause. The bewildering maze of contradiction, of difficulty involved, could hardly have been foreseen.

Mrs Florence Rutter had come to Australia to establish Soroptimist Clubs[1] for business and professional women, and it was while in Perth, her first Australian port of call, that her attention was drawn to the work of the child artists. Her determination to

[1] An organization originally founded in California, in 1921, complementary to Rotary Clubs for men.

FOREWORD

by

THE RIGHT REV. THE LORD BISHOP OF LONDON

THE Australian aboriginal is generally regarded as the representative of the most primitive type of culture the world of our day can still reveal. It is only too often concluded that he is therefore of a very low type of intelligence. Nothing could be farther from the truth. Those who have had occasion to take advantage of his skill in woodcraft have long recognized in him a particularly quick and observant mind, and those who have had to unravel his very complicated table of kindred and affinity have recognized that, where the computing of human relationships is concerned, he has his European brother completely beaten.

It is only in recent years that we have begun to understand that, given a fair opportunity, he can acquit himself honourably in academic and artistic spheres. We have scarcely got accustomed to the brilliance of Namatjiri's water-colours when news comes of the amazing development of a most delicate artistic skill among a group of aboriginal children in Western Australia.

In this book the story is beautifully told. It will arouse in us a sense both of achievement and of failure. The failure is the white man's, and it is none the less tragic because it is well-intentioned. One hopes that as a result of the publicity now given to the episode artistic skill will be given another chance and the social failure will be fully retrieved.

WM LONDIN

THE CARROLUP BOYS WITH THEIR TEACHERS

This photograph was taken on Florence Rutter's last visit to the school.

A GROUP OF GIRLS AT CARROLUP

With the girls are Prince Rudy Dinah, whose father was the last chief of the Bibbulman tribe, and Florence Rutter.

Mr and Mrs Noel White with Florence Rutter outside the School

visit their school had meant a tedious train journey to the south-western farming town of Katanning, 175 miles from Perth and a further twenty miles by car to the Carrolup native reserve.

The settlement consisted of a number of uncompromising stone buildings with iron roofs, rising bleakly from a sandy flat. In this inhospitable setting the warm greeting of the teachers, Mr and Mrs Noel White, had come as something of a surprise, but nothing equalling the intense surprise as they showed her the children's drawings on the school walls and took her round the settlement. A swift inspection had made it clear that living conditions provided for the children left much to be desired. The sleeping-quarters were drab, bare, and far from clean. Mattresses were grimy with the use of years. There were no pillows, and the covering—a single grey blanket to each bed—was patently inadequate. The children's clothing was shabby and soiled. Severe water shortage, she was told, prevented proper attention to cleanliness and hampered the teacher's lessons in hygiene.

It seemed a clear case for the committee and the busy bee, and what was the purpose of women's clubs if not to render assistance in such a cause?

Returning to Perth with a selection of pictures she had bought for her family and to exhibit on her travels, Mrs Rutter began to make inquiries. It was difficult, however, to receive simple answers to simple questions. Were the Australian people unmindful of their responsibility towards the first people of the land? It seemed that this was not entirely so. For the few who were prejudiced the many were sympathetic, but city people seldom, if ever, came into contact with aborigines, and felt that their needs were in the field of the specialist. Yes, a local committee would see to the dispatch of clothing to Carrolup if that would help at all, but, with so many causes within the white community, natives seemed rather out of the depth of the ordinary welfare-worker. This was really a matter for the Department of Native Affairs.

No one was able to explain satisfactorily how it was that after over fifty years of specialized native administration so little had been achieved towards helping the aboriginal to find a place in the community. Almost every one appeared to see the problem in the light of the particular facet with which he was familiar—and facets there were many. To some the 'aborigines' meant those natives still living under more or less original tribal conditions in remote, sparsely settled parts of the continent. These presented a different problem from the civilized or semi-civilized natives working for their keep or, in some cases, for regular wages on outback properties. There were natives on mission stations, who were another story altogether and different again from natives on Government settlements and reserves like Carrolup. Some still classed as aborigines the drifting, increasing population of mixed blood. Others contended that this section might better be classed, for the most part, as 'poor, mean white,' living under conditions approximating to the white slum.

All agreed, however, that there *was* a problem and that the fault lay somewhere. Perhaps, it was suggested, it lay in the nature of the aboriginal people themselves, who had rendered foolish and futile all efforts on their behalf since the beginning of Australian settlement. Some declared that the fault lay entirely with the Administration, but further inquiries indicated that this was, perhaps, too sweeping a statement. The Department, it seemed, was a body set up originally to protect the aboriginal people from exploitation or cruel treatment and later to formulate and administer a policy towards its charges. There were many different views. The fault lay with the public. The fault lay with the Government. The native should be assimilated. The native should be segregated. The natives were disappearing. The natives were increasing rapidly. Each statement seemed to cancel out another, and it was difficult for the stranger to perceive how there could be some truth in all.

Again and again Mrs Rutter endeavoured to bring the discussion back to the children of Carrolup.

"I realize there are these many problems, but I cannot hope to go deeply into them all. I can only undertake to help these young artists at Carrolup, and I should like to establish a few facts relating to their background."

But even so modest a demand had no simple answer, for the story of the children of Carrolup was the story of their race—a people betrayed by history into the hands of false gods.

CHAPTER TWO

CHILDREN OF 'DREAMING'

THE children of Carrolup were the remnants of many broken and vanishing tribes. A few waifs and strays had drifted down from the north or across from the vast desert stretches of the Nullabor Plain, to the east. Most, although they had no knowledge of it, were remnants of Australia's largest tribal group—the Bibbulmun, for Carrolup settlement itself lay in what was once the heart of Bibbulmun country, whose boundaries had embraced the fertile south-western triangle of the state, from Jurien Bay, 120 miles north of Perth, to the southern port of Esperance.

As with all Australian tribes, the unwritten history of the Bibbulmun is lost in antiquity, but it is thought that this—an isolated group, differing from others in certain practices—may have been a remnant of an earlier people, driven by fiercer, lustier invading hordes to seek shelter in the cold, spirit-haunted regions of the south.

The few songs and legends, salvaged from a dying culture, told of a time when they 'sat down' shivering in the forests, but how they lit great fires, warmed and comforted themselves, how the country 'knew them,' and they were glad.

By aboriginal standards this area was too cold for comfort, though it was a land of comparative plenty, of great waters and abundant food. They called it "Bibbulmun" ("many-breasts"), because the bounty of Nature flowed from the brown bosom of the land and many children were born to them. They had many women. There was no need here for the rigorous limitation of numbers that sanctioned the killing and eating of the newly born. Cannibalism, common to desert tribes, was countenanced only ritually in the rarest circumstances.

The Bibbulmun people lived principally on kangaroo, snakes, lizards, wallaby, fish, wild game, and witchetty grubs, supplemented by yams and other roots, their craving for sugar being assuaged by honey from wild bees and sometimes by honey from the base of flowers.

They were a gentle people. They sang long songs and dreamed long dreams, and the skins of furred animals, 'possums and kangaroos, worn as rough cloaks, protected them from the ravages of the southern winter. They crept into caves and hollow trees, or erected frail brushwood shelters when the driving winds and rains lashed the grey bush. Nomads of the virgin forest, they built no houses and sowed no crops, but their freedom of movement and conduct was limited by the barriers and taboos of unquestioned antiquity. The songs of the Bibbulmun throbbed with the pulse of the forefathers. Their lives flowed on in timeless reiteration of the unwritten past, ageless convention their rampart against destructive philosophies of progress and change.

At some time, farther back than the memory of man, the Bibbulmun had been divided into something over sixty family groups, each living within natural boundaries, rigorously observed. At first they had spoken the same language, but with the passage of time local variations and dialects sprang up, until at the coming of the white settlers the people of the most southerly families could scarcely make themselves understood by those of the other groups without recourse to the universal sign-language. They lived peaceably side by side, observing a code of reciprocal hospitality, a sharing of food in season, carried out under strict observance of age-old courtesy and tribal etiquette.

Such battles as they fought were brief affairs, resulting in a minimum of bloodshed for a maximum of noise and showmanship. The outcome of the 'war' was always decisive because the issue had been settled in advance at a conclave of old men. The elders knew well enough that youth must be allowed expression of its passions and the rigorous training of warriorship put to some apparent purpose, but they realized the futility of supposing such a pantomime capable of settling a dispute of political consequences. The feast at the close of hostilities involved all participants.

The initiation rites of Bibbulmun laid stress upon the relative unimportance of flesh, the indestructibility of spirit, and the perpetuation of mystic lore. They practised the ritual drinking of human blood, the intricacies of black magic, the preservation of sacred totemic articles, as did their more warlike neighbours, but they fought less and laughed more. Circumcision did not figure in their 'man-making' rites as with most tribes throughout the continent.

Women held a respected place in Bibbulmun society, sometimes rising in old age to a position of respect and power at least equal to the older men. The Bibbulmun weapons were less specialized, not so skilfully developed as in many parts of the continent, for ingenuity was less necessary where food was plentiful. Their tools were entirely of palæolithic time.

But, although their customs differed in many respects from those of other tribes, the Bibbulmun marriage laws, taboos, and 'skin' classes were Australia-wide, binding the wanderer, if such there was, to predestined associations and stylized modes of behaviour from coast to coast.

A son of the old people was at once a proud and a humble being, born as he was into a world of mysticism and symbolic rite in which every man became in his time the priest and guardian of cultural faith. His needs were simple, and his aspirations few beyond the gradual acquisition of esoteric philosophy. Personal possession, in the white man's sense, was a thing unknown, acquisition an unspoken heresy. Power was possible only through knowledge; knowledge, because of the carefully graded and widely spaced stages of initiation, possible only through age. Old men were the rulers of the race, high priests and administers of magic. This was a facet the white people would never understand. They spoke of native 'kings,' 'chiefs,' and 'sons of chiefs,' mistaking men of more powerful build and personality for the holders of rank unrecognized in the philosophy of Bibbulmun—or, indeed, in any Australian tribe.

The code by which all these first people of Australia lived was a quiet survival pattern, intricate in detail and complicated in structure, but essentially practical and in every detail maintained within their societies. There is little wonder that the white men, revered at first, were quickly summed up as hypocrites by a people who practised so literally and ritually what they preached. Generations of missionaries, zealous to uplift the heathen savage, to kindle the light of true faith in the darkness of his superstition, were to be foiled by the passive strength of the old beliefs, bewildered by the native's readiness to die when parted from the home of his spirit. Even to-day it is not fully realized how strong is the cord that binds the true-born aboriginal to his mother earth. His relationship to the soil and all life-forms that sprang from it was to him no poetic figure of speech. He did not possess his country, but was *possessed by it*. Plants, birds, and animals were his elder brothers, sometimes his ancestor gods, beloved as the relatives of his flesh and blood. Every member of the tribe was allotted at birth by a process of divination, not only a section of his country that was his spirit home—his '*dreaming*'—but his particular relatives in the plant and animal world. To him these were strictly taboo, and he would starve rather than eat the spirit brothers and sisters of totemic lore.

Ideas of conception, varying in detail throughout the continent, in principle remained the same. Man had emerged through a series of incarnations to his present state. It was not the highest, the ultimate, but just another stage, another form in an endless metamorphosis. The spirit of a child appeared to its father in a dream. It came in form of an animal, bird, or reptile. The father spoke of his dream. He would find the spirit again at some place to be remembered as its spirit home. Later the mother, perhaps bathing in a pool or passing a mound of stones, a rock, or a tree containing the spirits of children, would feel the child stir within her and know the prophecy fulfilled. In aboriginal belief no woman could conceive except by the lawful father of her child, who had first 'dreamed' its spirit in the form of its previous life.

To offer his wife or wives to the stranger was in aboriginal custom the merest hospitality—a friendly gesture of no possible consequence. On the coming of the white man it was quickly understood that this was not a custom of the strangers. The question of the aboriginal's expecting reciprocal hospitality in this sense seems never to have arisen, but his own women he offered freely and in innocence.

CHAPTER THREE

THE COMING OF THE DEAD

In ancient Bibbulmun belief the dead, on passing on to vaster regions of the unknown, rested at a certain 'Island of Souls,' known as Karrolup, which lay in the sea beyond sunset. Some times throughout the centuries spirits had returned from Karrolup in strange vessels and god-like raiment, and with awe and wonder the people of Bibbulmun had watched from afar, waiting a sign that they were the souls of their beloved dead returned. To all visitors since the time of Vlamingh, the Dutchman, in 1696, to that of Baudin, the Frenchman, in 1802, the people of the land had remained invisible, the only signs that there were inhabitants at all being footprints of astonishing size, a deserted whurlie,[1] and bellowing sounds, possibly of human origin. None of these early mariners had any good report to make of the thickly wooded country beyond Swan river. It might have been shunned indefinitely but for a certain enterprising young Scottish sea-captain, James Stirling, who came to Swan River on a voyage of investigation in 1827, when England was worried by reports of French and American warships cruising in the vicinity of the western coast.

Stirling, far from being repulsed by what he found, later reported it a "rich and romantic country," "a land, which of all I have seen . . . possesses the greatest natural attractions." He was enchanted by the smiling blue waters of his Black Swan river, its forest, scrub, and flowering creepers. The noise of the Bibbulmun 'thunder magic' dismayed him not at all. He penetrated as far as the river was navigable by small craft.

Old Yellagonga, elder of the river tribe, clearly recognized him as his dead son returned, for had he not given the sign in magically slaying the black swan—his son's totemic brother? With tear-

[1] A temporary shelter of bark, grass, and branches erected on a camp-site as a protection against sun and wind and used as sleeping-quarters in strict accordance with aboriginal family law.

stained cheeks and outstretched arms the old man ran to the water's edge.

"Nganna mammal!" ("My son!") It seemed to Yellagonga that his son had returned from the starry hunting-grounds of the heroic dead!

Stirling was impressed by the intelligence, general bearing, and hospitable attitude of these primitive hunters of Swan River.

"I cannot understand why others have given so poor an account of the aborigines," he wrote. "Their eyes are of extraordinary beauty and expressiveness and they have most excellent teeth."

Stirling came again in 1829 to found his Swan River colony. He was a just man, idealistic and kindly. He believed, in the beginning, that black and white could live together harmoniously, and he declared all aborigines subjects of his Majesty King George IV. The natives themselves believed they had nothing to fear from the *djanga*, the spirits of their dead returned. They watched, at first with respect and awe, but with growing mystification, the work of the colonists. The white men brought with them new laws, not only incomprehensible to their darker brethren, but against every tenet of their former faith. Humbly the Bibbulmun people gave up the fertile river frontages to the agriculturalist, and in due course helped themselves to the produce of the land. Misunderstandings grew to open warfare.

"These people," the colonists declared, "are Godless savages, without morality or respect of property. The colony cannot proceed unless they mend their ways."

One Yagan, a natural leader of his people, was decoyed into a boat, bound, and taken to an island where he was imprisoned in charge of a zealous and kindly colonist intent upon civilizing and converting him to Christianity. Yagan had quickly mastered the rudiments of the new language, and his conversations with the well-meaning Mr Lyon, carefully recorded in early newspapers, seem to have achieved no more than the conversion of his teacher to the consistency and simple logic of the aboriginal way of life.

There was nothing in the essential principles of Christianity which the people of Bibbulmun found difficult to understand. Indeed, all men were brothers, but brothers also of every life-form springing from a common soil. A native was permitted to kill for food, but taboos and totemic relationships reminded him always of the ties that bound him to the eternal rhythm of his universe. What was this new conceit that would place man above these creatures nurtured from the same soil, basking in the same sun, heir to the same spiritual cycle as the dark people of 'dreaming?' One loved one's neighbour as oneself. One did not kill outside the decree of ancient law. One did not steal—for what was stealing to a people without personal possession and within a law where no man went hungry when another feasted?

Lyon endeavoured to explain to his pupil that the black man must now learn to be provident and have thought for the morrow. But the old men from time immemorial had sung their songs of increase, thereby providing that the earth gave sustenance as it had from the beginning. It was evident that hoarding or personal acquisition led to ill-feeling between individuals and finally between tribes. Elaborate systems of hospitality and barter throughout the continent had provided against devastating warfare. Those who had within their territory an abundance of ochre, used for painting the dancers and their weapons on ceremonial occasions, bartered with those who could procure in their domain the emu-feathers used for similar purposes. And so it was with food. If a bad season befell one group it accepted the hospitality of another more fortunate. During long visits between tribes children were promised in marriage, within the complicated structure of inter-tribal relationships. Assuredly the law-givers had had thought for the morrow and all the to-morrows of their people as far as mind could reach.

Be that as it may, the black man must now forget his indolent way of life and work for sustenance! The black man laughed. Let the white man, then, stripped of all the trappings of civilization, scrounge a living from the Australian bush! Merely to survive was a matter of unremitting patience, endurance, and skill, and even as he sat in the shade in the heat of the day the aboriginal chipped and carved his precision instruments of the chase.

Yagan foiled his instructor at every turn and finally escaped to the mainland in a small rowing-boat with a single oar. After he was treacherously shot trouble with the tribesmen began in earnest. It became clear that these newcomers were not after all immortal and incorruptible spirits, but flesh and blood of another and an alien kind. They preached a law with their lips to which they did not adhere in their hearts. A cry went up from the camps of the Bibbulmun, "The smell of the *djanga* is killing us!"

Incensed and deeply disillusioned, the natives resorted to every form of sabotage. Brief periods of truce were always interrupted by further misunderstandings and retaliatory outrages, and finally it was Governor Stirling who, sorely tried and in fear of the future of his colony, led a party out in the hush of a winter's morning on a punitive expedition that shattered the spirit of Bibbulmun. They understood that from henceforth the white man was master in the land, that they existed now on sufferance on the hunting-grounds of their forefathers. They must henceforward wander homeless and without faith, a people without hope or pride or wish to live.

Despite a kindly effort to gather them together into a settlement, influenza and measles reduced their numbers almost to nothing. Farther south they survived only long enough to grieve for the days when their country 'knew them.' The natural boundaries that had divided group from group held no meaning now. The newcomers had parcelled out the country into small man-made lots, separating the dark people from their spirit homes and sacred waters.

Truly it could be said of a son of the Bibbulmun that he did not live by bread alone. No kindness or care could now replace those things of the spirit that he had lost. The new creed brought little comfort to a man who asked no more than to be a humble part of his country. Where was any meaning now since even mortal conception was no longer a phenomenon of mystical significance, since many children born to the shattered nomad families bore the pale stigma of their white overlords, until it was clearly seen that the dark race could survive only in a shadowy semblance of the forefathers, dark blood and white mingled but unreconciled.

The white man's god was all-powerful. He had torn the heroes of 'dreaming' out of the sky and the dark people must defer to him, though in their hearts they would recognize only the defeated spirits of the time past and with their dying breath whisper the chant-songs of Bibbulmun.

CHAPTER FOUR

THE YEARS BETWEEN

By the turn of the century the Bibbulmun, with their songs and stories, their gentle laughter and their sacred memories, had vanished from the face of the land. A few who had known and loved them mourned their passing, though it was felt to have been inevitable and it was believed that very soon their brothers throughout the continent must follow them.

The half-children of Bibbulmun were felt by black and white alike to be a thing of shame—a thing that never should have been and that was best ignored as far as possible. Some were killed in infancy, others were spared to be reared in the camps of a dying people in sorrow and humiliation. With the passing of the full-bloods they became a people apart, gipsies of the dusty country roads, to be pitied perhaps, but nowhere encouraged. In camel-carts and crazy horse-drawn vehicles they moved from place to place, nomads now less by nature than by force of circumstances. But there was pride in them still and in many the blood of robust pioneers whose names they often used. They were healthy and vigorous, and worked hard for their living in family groups. They asked no favours, expected no love outside the boundaries of their kind. Few though they were, they married strictly among themselves and with sorrow in their hearts watched a weaker, inbred generation grow up about them. Children of the wayside camps, these lacked stamina and stability, and showed little inclination to work if food could be obtained by begging. Drink became their currency. A people without pride, the women haunted the outskirts of country towns and the camps of lonely timber-cutters and railway fettlers. Their children, more virile through the further admixture of white blood, were lighter than themselves, and healthy enough, but they were still no more than shadows in the land. "A hopeless people," it was said, "a dying people. There is nothing one can do for them."

As it became evident that the aboriginal strain, neither negroid nor Mongolian, was progressively bred out it seemed that the problem might in time solve itself. But there was to be no such easy solution. True, girls from the native camps in casual association with white men produced near-white offspring who married white and became lost in the community, but these were the merest incidents. A people shunned and outcast, they were breeding for the most part among themselves, some even back into the aborigines from other parts of the state, producing a very brown Australian easily enough mistaken for full-blood at a casual glance.

If it was true that their aboriginal ancestors had, within the structure of their ancient faith, some form of thought for the morrow, these people assuredly had none. Honest attempts to employ them usually failed. The Department for Native Affairs, its duty being to shield a dying people from starvation and abuse, fended, fought, and even thought for them, taking over the function of their lost initiative. They became a people on the dole, drifting in grey bedraggled groups through the streets of country towns, barked at by dogs, 'warned off' by police. They had little enough left of native background—perhaps a few, half-remembered snatches of legend, superstition, or corroboree song, a smattering of native words. There were no culture heroes left in their sky, and only when it suited them to take what the missionaries offered did they bend their knees to another god. Exhorted to work and save, there seemed little point in either. Australia's generous child-endowment absolved whole families from the need to earn, encouraging them only in the will to increase.

The realization dawned at last that these people were neither dying out nor disappearing into the white community. In twenty or thirty years they had increased from a mere few hundred to over six thousand in the Great Southern District alone—an increase out of all proportion to that of the white community.

The idea of rendering the passing of a people easier had been well enough, but what now, since they had so ungraciously refused to co-operate? Even the full-blood had failed to disappear as quickly as had been predicted. It would seem we had mourned the passing of a people rather too soon, and that after all it was a progressive rather than a purely protective policy that was required.

But country communities and Road Boards[1] had no wish to provide building-sites for a derelict and unenlightened people who would quickly turn decent living-quarters into slums like those they already inhabited on the rubbish-dumps and sanitary reserves. Besides, building projects were expensive and materials, even for the white community, hard enough to come by. Why should they have things given them for which the respectable citizen had to work, save, and plan? "The natives must learn to want better conditions and to work for them of their own initiative," it was suggested.

This seemed a sound principle. There was no law against native children attending local schools, and the Department encouraged them to do so. Timidly the little darkies, conscious of audacity, shuffled into back desks. Shabby and unwashed, they hung their heads and made little progress. Protest meetings were held by outraged white parents who feared that their own children would become contaminated by these products of the rubbish-heaps. Native mothers tramped long distances with heavy buckets of water. They scrubbed their children and scrubbed their clothes and sent them off to school reasonably neat and clean. Some stood out and won the battle. The majority, hopeless and discouraged, fell by the wayside. Home conditions in shoddy huts were always against the children attaining much success, and so the vicious circle was maintained. No education without better living-conditions! No better living-conditions without education!

Missions there had been from the beginning of settlement, and, although they were able to do little to help the natives in the process of adjustment, they no doubt gave something to those who came within their range.

Government institutions endeavoured to cope with the most pathetic and degenerate. It was hoped that these establishments would become in time, not merely places of internment for 'unwanteds,' as they had begun, but well-organized training schools. There would be modern innovations of all kinds—good food, cottages for married couples, the best educational facilities. There was little they could do for the older people, but no doubt the children would show results. Many things were attempted throughout the years, and as in the case of the missions much

[1] Locally elected bodies which deal with civic matters pertaining to roads, water-supplies, sewerage, town-planning, etc.

alleviatory work was carried out. In time good hospital attention was provided, and here and there a model kindergarten was set up for the very young. Many good people brought love and enthusiasm to the task, but somewhere the seeds of failure lay in every endeavour. It was difficult enough to uphold a reasonable *status quo*, impossible to show progress in dealing with a situation that was as slippery as a snake, a people elusive as shadow. The settlements gathered together the young and the old, the healthy and the diseased, natives of all shades from full-bloods to near-whites. Children attending settlement schools spent their free time with the rogues and ne'er-do-wells of half a state and came to little good. The land granted for native reserves was always of the poorest kind. Water was inevitably short, and any agricultural project the Department might have planned was doomed to failure. Hopelessness and frustration lay like a fog upon the settlements.

Carrolup was established over thirty years ago to accommodate such problem cases as would have spoilt the chances of success for other institutions. There were sent the worst cases of congenital disease, the incorrigibles and inebriates, the incurable hospital cases. They were swept from missions and other Government reserves, from squalid camps and railway sidings, where they were a menace to the health and morals of country communities. Carrolup was a dumping-place for the human refuse of "Great Southern." A reserve of 5000 acres of inferior country 175 miles south of Perth, twenty miles off the main road from the nearest town, it was out of sight and mind of all right-thinking and fastidious people. The name, different in spelling from the 'Karrolup' referred to in early records of the Bibbulmun, was no doubt selected at random, and any association with lost souls was purely accidental.

CHAPTER FIVE

THE DARKNESS OF CARROLUP

A DEPARTMENT with the entire native problems of the state on its shoulders had little money or time to spare for the lot of the hopeless and the doomed. It did its best to obtain suitable staff, but the task was very difficult. Often enough a new superintendant, cook, or storekeeper would arrive on Tuesday's train and after a brief, despairing look round would take the return train on Thursday. For the most part the skeleton staff consisted of people who were unable to find better accommodation for a short period. Those few who came in a missionary spirit were usually forced to abandon the task because of the callous non-co-operation of their fellow-workers.

During the day the inmates drifted aimlessly about, only a few making inconsistent attempts to help. They ate and slept, laughed, wept, and quarrelled, while the very old and the very sick passed quietly away. Every evening at five, winter and summer, they were drafted into dingy, stone dormitories, where they cursed and fought and battered at the doors. They crowed like fowls and sang *The Prisoner's Song*. They slept in filth, inadequately covered in winter, stifling hot in summer. They were treated like wild animals and behaved appropriately, and even bars and barbed wire did not always succeed in keeping them in at night. Detention became a constant battle of wits between inmates and attendants.

Very occasionally, on the enthusiasm of a new staff-member or on threat of a Departmental visitor, there was some attempt to clean up, but the staunchest heart proved unequal to the task, and on those rare instances when an officer actually appeared he made no inspection of the native quarters. After all, what was the use?

As far as the general public was concerned the settlement was well placed. No road passed by. Nobody cared so long as this uncreditable legacy was kept well out of sight. But to the few who understood them the settlement people, although almost completely hopeless and recalcitrant, were not unlovable. The full-blood natives, even those sent there on charges of disorderly conduct, assault, or thieving, were for the most part gentle and easy to handle. The mixed-bloods were a more difficult proposition. With many characteristics of the aborigine, they had others that were the result of race mixture and confusing environment. They had grown to demand and expect everything for nothing. They said thank you, but the words carried no sense of gratitude. The presenting of little gifts—"tokens," they called them—they practised and understood as being some form of payment or discharge of obligation. The 'gift' might be a bunch of withered flowers, a bird's egg, a few feathers, a roughly carved boomerang. It was the gesture, not the value, one was expected to acknowledge. It was said that work for these people was a "thankless task," and this was true enough if one looked for thanks. That "they always let you down" was equally true. Here was no place for those who feared disappointment or cherished illusions too dearly.

Capable of strong attachment, sometimes even devotion, they were seldom weighed down by loyalty in the sense we use the word. However kind a previous superintendent or staff-member, few natives would hesitate, if it suited their ends, to convey the impression that they had suffered persecution under his régime. The innocent gaze bestowed upon the questioner, far from being an indication of frankness and ingenuousness, was likely as not a shrewd appraisal of the expected or desired answer. Past-masters of the art of mime, it was not necessary to defame or praise a character in so many words. A glance, an inflexion of the voice, and the impression—for good or ill, and usually to the complete satisfaction of the uninitiated—was conveyed.

They harboured little resentment, though some indulged in passionate outbursts of anger against the white man, fierce avowals of the dark man's superiority, the white man's meanness and cruelty. They showed no repentance for wrongdoing and had little sense of shame in the white man's meaning of the word. They lied constantly and unfalteringly, but had no respect for the man or woman who accepted the lie. They laughed when their deceit was discovered and expected the white man to laugh too. They expected no punishment and showed little dread of it. The 'boob,' the small, dark cell to which the most uncontrollable

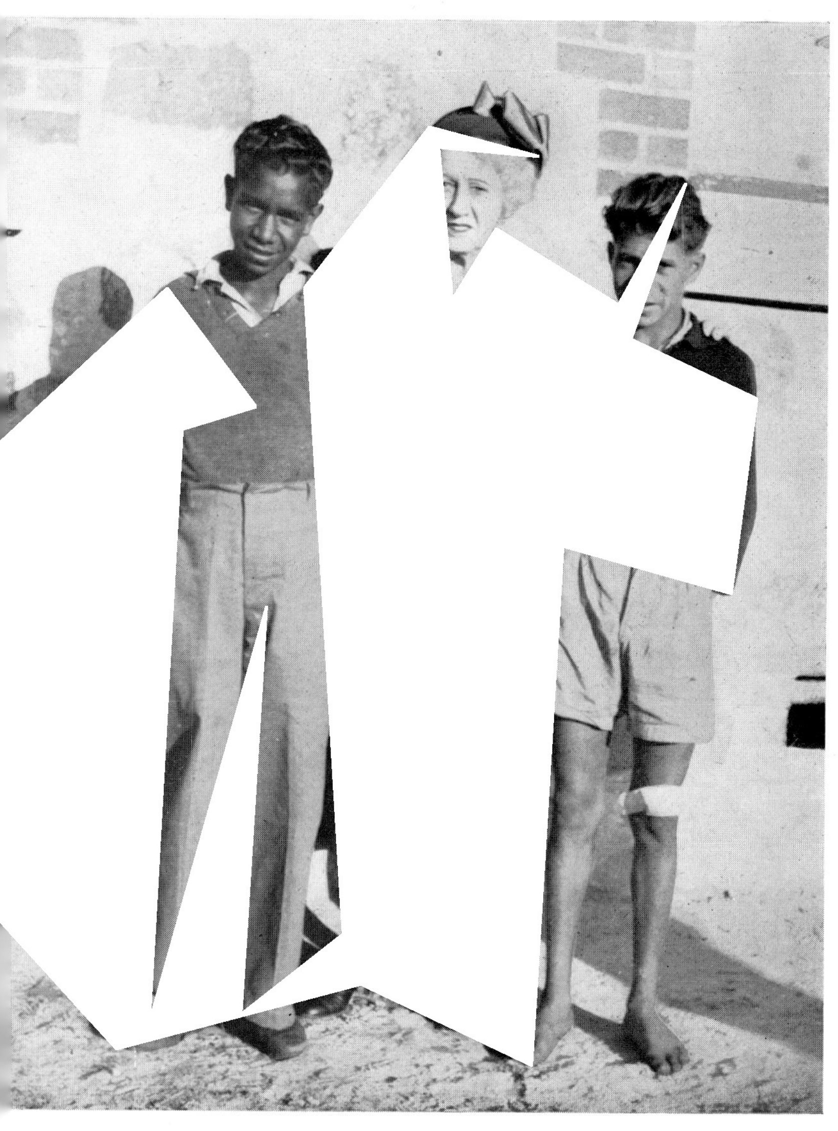

TWO OF THE BOYS TAKEN WITH FLORENCE RUTTER ON HER FIRST VISIT TO CARROLUP NATIVE SETTLEMENT

Left, Reynold Hart (14 years), a full-blood aboriginal. *Right*, Parnell Dempster (13 years), a half-caste aboriginal.

THREE OF THE ARTISTS SHOWING THEIR FIRST DRAWINGS IN FRENCH PASTEL
They found no difficulty in working with this new medium. The boy in the centre is Parnell Dempster.

were consigned, was no great hardship. So long as food was forthcoming—which was usually the case—they could sleep the clock round and like it. They were not lacking in respect for other men's creeds, although few professed any of their own. They never mocked the weak or unfortunate. Old age and deformity was respected, in a sense, perhaps loved, though love in our sense was not common among them. There was love, certainly, for the child, the parent, the blood-relative. These bonds were true and strong, even passionate, and they carried loyalty too, but such emotions seldom extended to sex relationships. There was little desire for steady married life or, indeed, marriage in any form. This seemed to the average native, man and woman alike, an altogether false and unnatural bondage. The passing association, yes—passion and violence. It was a poor lover who did not, at some time, split his woman's head; but to be tied to one man or one woman—that was surely intolerable? And to what possible advantage could it be in a society where there were no homes to be made, no future to be planned for? But fatherhood was acknowledged and carefully remembered. A coloured woman would have little reticence in revealing the various fathers of her half-dozen offspring.

The population of Carrolup was for ever changing—new people coming in on warrant, others being discharged or simply running away and being brought back. Patients came and went and came again. Girls came to have their babies and returned to their places of employment or their squalid home-camps, sometimes leaving the baby to be cared for at the settlement. Relatives came on visits; indigents drifted in and out. It was not all unhappiness. There were good times in the camp. Sometimes there was laughter and play almost in the old corroboree spirit of former days, ending up in traditional fashion with split heads and bad bruises. But the good times were inevitably complicated by the drink that in the face of all regulations to the contrary was somehow spirited into the settlement.

As time went on the children of Carrolup had become an increasing problem. A school of sorts was established, a cheerless stone building with a cement floor and a minimum of equipment. It was hardly likely that "these the least of His brethren" would be capable of imbibing much benefit from the innovation —a little reading and writing perhaps, and the most elementary arithmetic. Now that such sick and delinquent children as were not acceptable to other institutions had been sent to swell the child population of Carrolup at least some attempt must be made to keep them out of mischief.

Only one qualified teacher had preceded Mr and Mrs White to the settlement school, and she—brave woman though she was—had admitted the task to be beyond her strength. It was a chance meeting with her in 1945 that had first drawn the attention of Mr White and his wife to the need of the Carrolup children. Mrs Elliot had spared them no details as to the conditions at the settlement. The teacher's house, she explained, was a rickety iron shack—an oven in summer, cheerless and draughty in winter. There was little furniture—a packing-case for a table, boxes for chairs. There was neither bathroom nor laundry. The 'kitchen' was a small stove in the open. Water was scarce and at best brackish, and the only light supplied by the Department was one hurricane lantern.

Perhaps it was true that little could be done for the older natives at the settlement, but the children, Mrs Elliot pleaded, were surely not to be abandoned! She had felt at times that there was some promise there—rare glimmerings of interest and intelligence—but the establishment was so lacking in any form of hygiene or discipline that it was beyond the power of a woman, with a small daughter of her own, to progress very far. Many of her pupils were big, strapping, riotous boys and girls who needed a man to manage them. She appealed to Mr White: "They have nothing in the world—no hope, no future. Perhaps you could give them *something*!"

Mr White admitted to some experience of aboriginal pupils, but he explained that the Carrolup children presented a very different problem from those he had known in other country schools.

His first contact with aborigines dated back to 1930, when as a very young man he was appointed head teacher of a small school in the little gold-mining town at Payne's Find. This settlement of the Lower Murchison district, a hundred miles from the nearest railway, was set away in the mulga country north of Perth, its inhabitants hardy prospectors and a floating population of aborigines.

Mr White had viewed the darkies with detached interest on his arrival, but when he opened the school he was amazed to find only one white boy in a class of forty or fifty coloured children ranging from full-bloods to quarter-castes. At first his reactions were somewhat confused, and he was forced to remind himself that the educationist must observe no social boundaries. But these children, different from the waifs of Carrolup, were born of self-respecting coloured parents who earned their livings by trapping foxes and kangaroos or working on stations as boundary riders, stock-drovers, or shearers, and in some cases as prospectors. They were, no doubt, in the same stage of robust independance as the 'first cross' of Bibbulmun and white man in the earlier settled regions farther south. None of these families received any assistance from the Government in the way of food or clothing. They had pride of race and a deal of self-respect. The children, timid at first, were well-mannered, clean, and willing to learn, and their teacher soon found that in singing, poetry, and all forms of manual and artistic expression they excelled the ordinary class of white children. It was traditional among them to carve pictures on emu eggs. Scraping through the thick green outer shell to the white beneath, they carved bush animals, native weapons, and sometimes trees and little landscapes. The more ambitious made remarkable carvings in the hard mulga-wood, whose twisted roots and branches often suggested, before the days of Henry Moore, birds, reptiles, and animals. Many of these children, now men and women scattered through the countryside, owe their liberal education and much of the respect in which they are held in the community to the five years of patience and understanding bestowed on them by Mr White.

Now, recalling this experience, he was stirred, with the support of his wife, to do what he could for the children of Carrolup. They applied and were accepted for the onerous post.

Here indeed was a very different state of affairs from that which had confronted the young teacher at Payne's Find. These were the children of mendicants who knew no way of living other than that of begging and vagabondage. They had come a long way from the proud, hunting forefathers of the primeval forests.

CHAPTER SIX

A LIGHT IS KINDLED

THE children had eyed the new teachers suspiciously. They were already past-masters of the art of discouraging unwelcome staff. If mass riotousness failed, a solid phalanx of stubborn non-co-operation, sullenness, and impenetrable stupidity usually proved invincible.

Mr and Mrs White also took careful stock of their pupils. By and large the children did not look such an unpromising bunch. Under the simulated mask of sullenness and the grimy hallmarks of neglect it was obvious that the majority had bright-enough faces, good teeth, and for the most part, when not infected by flies and filth, eyes that were large and soft as those of the kangaroos of their native country. Like kangaroos, too, they were wild, fleet, and shy.

There were people the aborigines unaccountably rejected and despised; there were those they feared and those they tolerated; there was a few—one or two in a lifetime, perhaps—whom they would follow to the grave. Whatever the characteristics required for this type of leadership, Mr White assuredly possessed them in full measure. A commanding glance, a wave of his flexible hands, and their riotousness was quelled. Fun and laughter he allowed them in full measure, though he knew well enough that they must be allowed to laugh *with*, not at, their teachers, or the day was lost. He was fair and firm, and, whatever may have been his feelings in the first few months, he somehow infused into his class-room a feeling of confidence and optimism. He may, as has been suggested, have unconsciously exerted some vital personal magnetism over his pupils, something of the influence of a Svengali over his Trilby. However it was, the children worshipped him.

A few of his Carrolup pupils were full-blood aborigines from various parts of the state. The rest ranged in colour from almost black to almost white. One or two were further complicated by a streak of Chinese and one, at least, by a dash of Negro, but aboriginal was a common denominator, and at a casual glance most might readily enough have been summed up as 'black.' All were totally untrained in deportment and the rudiments of hygiene. At first when spoken to they hung their heads and turned away, and it was impossible to assess the average intelligence of the school as anything but low. It was difficult to know where to begin and how to create an interest in anything at all.

Not the least difficulty in teaching the children to be clean was the shortage of water and the defeatist attitude on the part of the existing white staff. The children had the normal youngster's distrust of cold water and soap, but after a deal of tactful manœuvring a system was inaugurated whereby they were enabled to combine hygiene with the necessary quota of fun. They made a fire in the open, set a kerosene-tin of water over it, and, amid screams, squeals, and splashing, scrubbed each other vigorously.

With an improving Departmental attitude good food was not denied at Carrolup. A case of fruit a day, oranges and apples in season, were allowed the children. These the teacher handed out at playtime, and as they filed up any who had obviously dodged the kerosene-tin ritual missed that day's ration. In very short time this first lesson had been learned.

Realizing that the first essential was to win the children's confidence, Mr White dispensed with a formal time-table for the first month or two. Acting on the advice of the Education Department district inspector, Mr Crabbe, whose kindly understanding of native children and their special problems was well known throughout the state, Mr White determined to find a starting point in those arts and activities connected with native life. The song, the dance, the dramatization of simple stories, animal impersonation—these things were close to them still and had formed part of their broken, wandering, sometimes hunted lives.

In the knowledge that "music hath charms," Mr White produced his flute, and a magic instrument indeed it proved to be. When he was at Payne's Find he had observed that there were two pitches to the native voice—one that was harsh and ugly, another that was soft, sweet, and true. He taught them to use only the pleasing one. Soon they were singing in unison, two parts, and rounds, always with great feeling and enjoyment. School inspectors who visited Carrolup from time to time later declared that they could never hear these songs without emotion. "They could impart something wistful to their singing," one officer recorded. "The effect was unforgetable as were their faces as they sang, their dark eyes, large and luminous, fixed upon their teacher."

And then the dance! Mr White almost despaired at first as the children pushed, scrambled, and shoved, noisy and ill-mannered. Gradually, with an increasing desire to please and to succeed, coupled with a natural sense of rhythm, they were dancing delightfully, not only their own native corroborees, but also English folk-dances.

These small successes were a great source of inspiration and encouragement to their teachers, but there were times too of deep sadness and despondency. All their efforts were hampered by the fact that there had never been at any time a clear-cut policy as to the future. The children would leave school at fourteen to fare as best they could. No one—not the Department of Native Affairs nor the Department of Education, certainly not the children themselves—had the least idea for what they were being educated. To have suggested that the girls were to be trained and educated as domestics would have been considered somehow shocking in a democratic country, though this was in fact the *best* they could hope for under existing circumstances. Nor was it ever stated that the boys were to be trained to work on farms or timber-mills. This too would have appeared undemocratic, even dangerous, though with the little education they received they were seldom fitted to be even very reliable labourers. "A gradual improvement of standards—a building up of confidence" was as near as Mr White could get when he inquired as to what was required of him, but he knew that any standards he built up would be quickly broken down when, at the tender age of fourteen, his pupils, sent out to battle in a hard, cold world, realized that they were only natives after all, that the colour of their skin proclaimed them the perpetuation of an ancient national sin—the blending of black blood with white.

Mr White realized that the age of fourteen was the most critical of all in the life of a coloured child. If it was important for a white child to receive guidance and direction at this time, it was even more so in the case of the native. How often he had heard it said. "They learn all right up to fourteen and then their minds seem to close up." It was precisely at this time that the coloured children began to realize their place, or, rather, lack of place, in the community. Emotional 'blockages' caused serious consequences often resulting in delinquency and vandalism. Mr White decided that he must at least teach his pupils to be well mannered, to speak and sing pleasantly, to read, write, and compose letters sufficient for some problematic future spent in native camps or in a limited selection of possible employment. He could not contemplate embarking them on a full or normal curriculum. Their experiences, from a point of view of taking a place in a white man's world, were extremely limited. They had known no normal homes or home influences. Books, even comics, were scarcely known to them. They knew the district or districts in which they had wandered, but beyond that lay the great unknown—a void whose significance never in any way impinged upon their consciousness.

Almost the greatest difficulty was the children's extreme shyness and sensitiveness. Even when deliberate obstinacy had been overcome and they were singing and dancing with some confidence they were otherwise inarticulate. Their teachers tried to fill some of the gaps in their experiences by stories and pictures, encouraging them to talk over and act simple incidents. Gradually they succeeded in unlocking the lips of their pupils, a process tremendously and at first unexpectedly assisted by their art.

Here we come to a matter of vital significance and ever-increasing interest. Many theories have been and will continue to be advanced as to the source and development of the extraordinary work these children produced. It has therefore been important, before the whole story becomes confused in memory and legend, to gather a few facts concerning the beginnings and growth of their artistic achievements. Without certain important clues theories can be only hazy and tentative.

Some believe that Mr White must assuredly have been an artist himself, others that there was probably *one* talented boy, whom the rest copied. Still others maintain that the children learned nothing except how to paint. The validity of any of these opinions the reader can judge for himself on the few essential facts provided. A search back into old files and records revealed a few of the children's work-books from the brief and broken period of schooling they had received before the coming of Mr and Mrs White. The books were grubby and without anything to indicate especial talent in any of the children. Even the best, that of Reynold Hart, was of a low standard. He had drawn the things school-children are traditionally given to draw, though in his case they were objects he was hardly likely ever to have seen—a lighthouse, a much-blurred and bescribbled sea, some birds probably copied from overseas text-books, a robin, a thrush perched on the sort of trees young children conventionally draw with round masses for foliage.

Almost abruptly the tune changed to the extent that the children began to depict—crudely enough, but with more attention to cleanliness—nature subjects with which they were familiar.

Mr White started them on 'scribble' patterns, encouraging them to scribble over the page and fill in the spaces with different colours. He was surprised to find that the children carried this idea beyond his expectations, forming patterns and efforts quite different from and more interesting than those of white children of his experience. On his first visit to Carrolup Mr Crabbe was also struck with this fact.[1]

Mr Crabbe had examined Mr White when he taught in a small school near Geraldton, and had been struck then with this teacher's musical ability and gift for encouraging singing and rhythmic dancing. Here Mr White had run an obviously happy school of good general standard, but his pupils, though he had encouraged them to record their observations in nature study, had exhibited no particular flowering in art. Realizing that his ability from an art teaching point of view was limited, Mr Crabbe—no mean artist himself—suggested how the children's expression might be encouraged further.

As it was not possible in those early stages to know how much of the lesson the children had taken in it was suggested that they should attempt to sketch what they had learned. The results were humorous, but again surprisingly alive. Mr White pursued the idea into simple history, geography, and nature-study lessons, and was encouraged at the keenness of observation their sketches revealed.

Even so, the general condition at the settlement seemed such as would never allow the children any chance of ordinary progress. The good work undertaken in school hours was offset by association with the many older inmates. Little help was forthcoming from the average staff-members, who, anxious to escape the oppressive atmosphere of the settlement, dispersed almost every

[1] A few years later he was to see a similar result from the introduction of scribble patterns to a class of native children in the north-western port of Derby, though time did not allow his following up his observations.

evening to the nearest township. As all their charges were well under lock and key by five o'clock they no doubt felt that their day's work was over. Many returned with drink, which was usually 'smelt out' and pillaged next day, setting up a constant atmosphere of suspicion and enmity between staff and inmates.

Mr and Mrs White as employees of the Educational Department were expected to devote themselves exclusively to the education of the children. Any interference with affairs that concerned the superintendent and staff was severely frowned upon. Sometimes, however, interference was unavoidable. One stifling summer's night Mr White was aroused by the sound of more than usually frantic noises from the girls' dormitory, and, hurrying from his house, found the children fighting to get to the small barred window. Clouds of smoke were pouring from the room. The dormitory attendant who kept the keys was not on duty. Mr White broke the door open with an axe in time to prevent a tragedy. The children fell out, gasping and with streaming eyes, and confessed how one of them, smoking a forbidden cigarette, had set her mattress alight.

Soon after this incident Mr White obtained permission from headquarters for a section of the children to be permitted each evening to play outdoor games for a couple of hours. This blessed reprieve from the five-o'clock curfew was accepted with glee. Mr White encouraged the children to practise competitive sports at this time, and he was surprised one evening to receive a deputation from a group of boys. Parnell Dempster had been appointed spokesman.

"Show us a light, sir, please! We fellas like to make some picture like in school."

"You want a light in the schoolroom?"

The boy grinned shyly. "That's right, sir!"

CHAPTER SEVEN

NEW ERA

It would seem that from this time a new era had dawned for the children of Carrolup. Gone the terrible dreariness of the long evenings, shut up in dark dormitories with nothing to do but devise ways and means of getting out or of finding something to wreck in the almost bare and gloomy prison. Now, with touching eagerness, they crowded to the schoolroom after dark, gathering to the light of a single hurricane lantern. Hungrily, almost greedily, they used the time that had been given them.

"Perhaps a first enthusiasm," Mr White warned his wife. "They may get tired of it."

But the children never tired. Night after night the enthusiasm grew as the wall-space was filled with pictures. At bedtime Mrs White would come with supper—tea or cocoa, little cakes, bread and jam. Sometimes they sang for a while, sometimes sat on discussing their work and their plans.

Superintendents and other staff-members came and went in monotonous succession. Some were kindly and co-operative to the teachers, sending the children off clean to school, providing good meals and medical attention. Others, perhaps resentful at the suggestion that everything was not up to the mark, jealous of the teachers' influence over the children, were anything but helpful, often insisting on the right to call certain pupils out of class on sanitary or wood-cutting fatigue—a fact responsible for greatly retarding the progress of the most willing and diligent boys.

Heart-breaks and disappointments were many in the teachers' lives, but their work went on. Slowly habits of hygiene and deportment were formed, and the children gained confidence and self-respect. The better pupils, about six of the older boys, were now using large sheets of brown or cartridge paper, Mr White having observed that a large sheet encouraged expression. They were beginning to depict sunset scenes, they were showing a liking for skeleton trees and autumn shades, and they were introducing birds and animals into their pictures. Mr White, however, was puzzled and somewhat troubled at the children's growing tendency to what he feared might be a careless linear development.

"I'm afraid you'll be disappointed in this, sir," he said apologetically on the occasion of Mr Crabbe's next visit. The inspector examined the sketches carefully and pronounced judgment.

"There's something quite new and remarkable coming out here. Leave their style alone. Just go on encouraging their interest and observation!"

Any actual instruction they received in the use of media was from Mr Crabbe during his brief, very occasional visits. In the second year of their art development he showed them how to apply a graded wash and how it was possible to draw with the brush, though he was sensitive lest he should hamper them with directions or in any way interfere with the characteristic style they were developing. Those who seek a clue to the origin of this style will not find it in Mr Crabbe's own delicate, academically finished paintings.

The children quickly adapted suggestions to a technique of their own, amazing their teachers by their adeptness with their brushes. They appeared to move and develop in a group, through a process of mutual interest, discussion, and criticism, though it was found that artistic ability was here correlated very directly with intelligence. The brighter children produced the best artwork. In this particular group the children of part-white blood were better scholars and artists than the few full-blood aborigines, though this fact cannot be taken as axiomatic of Australian colour differences generally. The girls showed little initiative beyond the scribble patterns, though in many of these they produced lively and original results.

It did not occur to Mr and Mrs White until their pupils' art began to attract the amazed attention of educational authorities, that the work might have some merit *of itself*. So far they had merely used a natural facility as an aid to interest and understanding and to quicken already keen senses of observation. As time went on the two teachers confessed that they felt somewhat out of their depth in many of the discussions evoked by the children's work. Sometimes they found themselves being cross-examined almost belligerently as though they were suspected of a form of charlatanry or trickery.

"Now come, Mr White! How much of this work did you actually *do yourself*? . . . It's ridiculous, then, to say they're untaught?"

"Oh, yes!" Mr White would explain patiently. "Mr Crabbe gave them a full hour's instruction on how to use their brushes when he was here four months ago."

"Ah! And you, of course—*influenced* them?"

"Certainly I did! I influenced them to use the eyes in their heads. Sometimes I would take them back and back to the same place, even to the same tree, to see how things looked at different times of the day, in different lights. When they made their first tentative sketches of trees I would encourage them but I would suggest also that we went for another walk to find out more about the way branches grew from trunks and how foliage masses looked against the sky."

Soon, he explained, he realized that the children noticed more detail than he himself did, remarking on the peculiar shapes and patterns of peeling bark, of tree hollows and bumps. Their visual memory developed in the classroom what they had seen on their walks. In a short time they were sketching, with varying success, the spindly York gums with their fan-shaped foliage, the queer primeval shapes of the 'blackboys,' or grass-trees, with their thick, blackened stems, shock-haired foliage, and towering flower-spikes.

The children talked with increasing animation of trees and landscapes, of sunset and moonlight, of sunshine and shadow, of animals and birds. Their sight, always keen, was used now to a new purpose. Sometimes they would go for night walks with their teacher, and great was their delight to discover an owl or a 'possum thrown in silhouette against a full moon. They could not return quickly enough to record their discovery in water-colour and pastel.

Mr White hardly remembers when real perspective first came into the children's work. Here they undoubtedly have been influenced by the picture-books their teachers had by this time collected for them. The boys, however, without realizing that they were solving weighty problems of perspective, often discussed their observations.

"You *think* the road goes small, only when you walk on it's the same all the way."

"Fences too!" another would contribute. "You think the posts go small!"

Later they tried out this discovery and announced triumphantly:

"You want to draw how you *see*, not how you *know*!"

Gradually the drawings expressed individuality and character. The children's writing also developed. Illustrations in nature-study and hygiene books were explained by notes in careful printing. All their books were amazingly neat and clean. Soon they were depicting the life stories of Australian birds and animals, adding to the pictures little descriptions and remarks of their own.

"Notice the tough and big tail of the kangaroo! He depends on this tail to give him balance."

"The old man 'possum sits still on a waving branch, fearing nothing."

"Notice the lovely look on the 'possum's face and the bright twinkle in his eye. The 'possum's tail is very useful. Without it he can't climb very good."

When he first came to the settlement Mr White had noticed an unthinking tendency towards cruelty to bush creatures, and he had spoken to the children of the bush native's gentleness and love of animals, how they killed for food, but never teased or tortured, how 'joeys' were often taken from the pouch of a dead doe kangaroo, were lovingly cared for, and brought up as pets in the camp. The children listened attentively and developed a love of the bush creatures, carefully observing every detail of movement and habit.

They collected examples of native timbers, carved, cut, or polished them, and produced many beautiful inlaid trays and platters. The girls too were interested and were remarkably good at handicrafts. During the War they gave some lovely pieces of work to the Red Cross. The boys sketched designs on cushion- and chair-covers, and these the girls worked, tapestry fashion, in startling colours. These they gave either to charity or to people who had shown them especial encouragement or kindness. The like of these rare pieces of needlework design have never been done elsewhere, and if it were now possible to produce them should be preserved as national treasures. Boys and girls alike felt them to be important and especially precious, as the following little story indicates.

A fourteen-year-old native girl who helped Mrs White with the younger children was directing the production of a cushion-cover resplendent with corroboree figures dancing about a camp fire. This girl was one day brought before the matron to have her hair cut short in a style to which she objected, and in the scuffle that ensued the scissors penetrated the matron's arm. Consternation reigned at Carrolup! The girl was convicted of assault and was taken away to serve her sentence in Fremantle gaol, her age having been given as sixteen at the time of her trial. She was less concerned about the actual charge and sentence than about the precious cushion-cover, and she tearfully begged Mrs White to see that no mistakes were made during her absence. After strenuous representations from understanding friends the girl was released at the end of one week and returned triumphantly to finish the sacred task in time for Christmas.

Quickly the children ventured into more complicated forms of artistic expression. Sometimes while they worked Mr White would read them verses from the Australian ballad poets, and these too were translated into pictures.

> The colours of the setting sun
> Withdrew across the Western land.

Here was a word-picture they understood, and soon it was seen with what delight and intensity they had observed the rich, kaleidoscopic skies of Australian sunset—the rose, the scarlet, the yellow, and the green.

> The lustrous purple blackness of the soft Australian night
> Waned in the grey awakening that heralded the light.

Dawn and the waning stars between the intricate branches of the slim bush trees! These children of wandering families, who had slept in the open often as not, were familiar with all the subtleties of moonlight, darkness, and dawn. Increasingly their pictures showed a love and understanding of the bush, derived no doubt from their tribal ancestors—the old people of whom they seldom spoke except in terms of disparagement. "Noongars" ("poor bush-blacks") they called them, while the white people were "Wadjelars" ("great white ones")

Quietly Mr White told them of the tribesmen of bygone days, how they had been a proud and happy people, ideally adapted to their environment, explaining that there was no cause for shame in their native ancestors. He told of how John Eyre crossed the vast Nullabor Plain with his faithful boy Wylie, of Sir John Forest's devoted and beloved Tommy Winditch and of all the nameless and unsung who succoured perishing explorers, who helped the pioneers to build their homes in the wilderness, shepherded their flocks, and guarded their families. He spoke too of Albert Namatjira, the Central Australian aboriginal whose paintings were now famous; he told also what he knew of the native way of life before the coming of the white man. He encouraged them to imbibe as much of their own folk-lore as possible from the few full-blood natives who drifted in and out of the settlement.

Hitherto the children had been half ashamed of their interest in the stories of the old people and had talked with them surreptitiously. Now they gathered happily round their camp-fires, learning the stories, almost forgotten, of the fine old tribes, following the words and movements of corroborees and ceremonial dances.[1] They learned how the warriors of old had arrayed themselves for sacred occasions, of the weapons that had been used in the hunting-days, how the bush people had stalked and killed their prey.

From their own people they learned that which no white man could teach them—the deep, aboriginal feeling for country, a sense of mysticism and ancient magic, which they infused into many of their pictures.

These old people of Carrolup, broken-down and derelict though they mostly were, brought the 'dream time' of aboriginal belief to life for the children of another age, and it is to their influence that must be attributed the pictures of native life, of corroboree and hunting and totemic decoration.

[1] The word 'corroboree' appears to have been introduced by the early settlers and is not actually native in origin. Loosely used, it refers more properly to the purely social dances, which include mime, animal imitation, mimicry, drama, and comedy. Ceremonial dances are of a religious nature, solemn, awe-inspiring, and usually for the initiates only.

CHAPTER EIGHT

CARROLUP COMES TO TOWN

THE children had long since ceased to be a difficult and backward group and had emerged as interesting individuals. Many had interesting, sometimes heart-rending, stories of wandering and neglect, though they seem to have taken everything very much as a matter of course—camp life, settlement life, mission life. They had, at least, never starved and never lacked companionship. Most had a good idea of their immediate antecedents and of their individual percentages of black and white blood. In many instances they had selected their own surnames for the purpose of the school register. Few of the parents, with the exception of an occasional forgotten white father, were quite regardless of their children's welfare. They usually managed to keep in touch through messages delivered by friends and relatives or by personal visits. In some cases the mother—unmarried, widowed, or deserted, and working on some outback farm—had been glad enough to leave her elder children in the sympathetic hands of good teachers. Time was when the very mention of Carrolup had caused shiftless native parents to mend their ways, but now word had spread about that things were different, and parents with vague dreams of better things for their little ones sent them off willingly enough to Mr and Mrs White.

Inspectors had already taken some of Reynold Hart's exercise-books, scrupulously neat and clean, for display to other schools. All Reynold's work was of a high standard, and he himself had been quick to learn lessons of cleanliness and deportment. Gentle, alert, and intelligent, he attracted the attention and commendation of inspectors and other visitors. Reynold was probably the brightest in his group from an intellectual point of view, and many consider his work to have somewhat excelled the rest.

Revel Cooper probably ran him a close second. In many respects Revel's work was more imaginative, though on the whole it lacked the painstaking finish of the quieter and more gentle

THE 'POSSUM

A large pen-and-ink drawing (18 by 24 in.) by Revel Cooper.

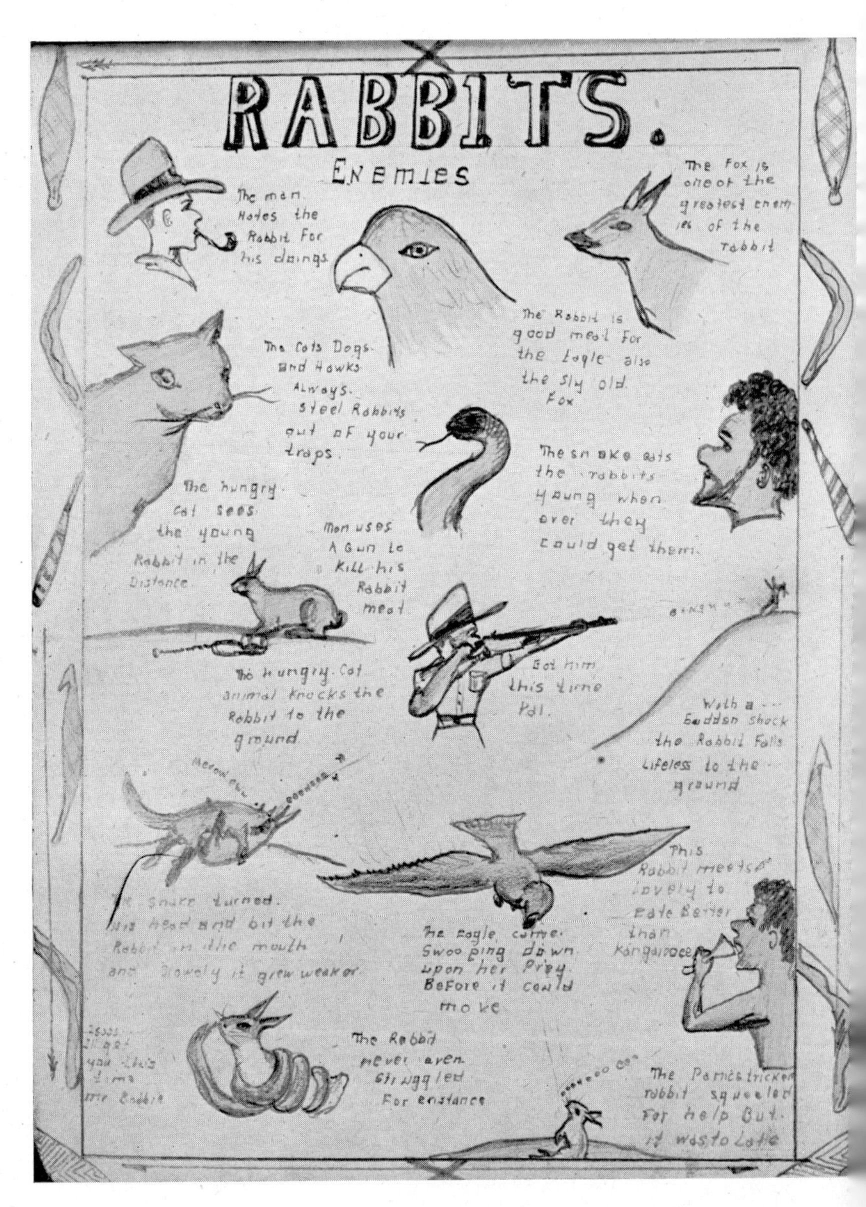

RABBITS

Another page from Revel Cooper's book, describing the enemies of the rabbit. Among the enemies are both white settlers and natives.

Reynold. Revel was a strong, burly lad of vital, volatile, and artistic temperament. He and Barry Loo were perhaps the most ambitious of the group. Barry, a good-looking, rather reserved boy, showed great promise at this time, though he was not as easy to know and understand as most of his companions. Shrewd, sensitive, and proud, he was somewhat slower to give trust and confidence, and his teachers found themselves wondering how he would fare in a world that still looked for a measure of subservience in its coloured people.

Parnell Dempster, no doubt owing to a somewhat chequered career, was no star scholar, but his good nature and co-operation were indispensible to his teachers. Although one of the most talented young artists, he showed no desire to excel his companions. His ambition wavered, at this time, between wanting to become a baker and yearning to drive a wheat-lorry.

Claude Kelly, a tall young stripling, was also producing some outstanding art-work, though his unfortunate background seemed likely always to exercise an unstabilizing effect on his career. His health and eyesight also were indifferent.

Cliff Ryder's name was appearing on some of the best pictures, and his manual work, at a country show, had been judged the best of any school child in the Katanning district. A serious, sincere, boy, he listened attentively to his lessons, always intent upon pleasing and doing the right thing.

The different children showed individual tastes in choice of colours and subjects. Barry Loo's work, for instance, could always be distinguished by his use of a peculiar shade of peacock-green, a colour he would make a dive for in the box before any other. Both Reynold Hart and Revel Cooper liked to throw their trees out in startling silhouette against blazing sunset skies. Cliff Ryder indefatigably sought out and depicted dead or ring barked trees. Parnell Dempster excelled at night scenes. If there was a tendency among the less-gifted children to echo the successes of the better artists there seems no strong evidence of one or two particular boys dominating the artistic development of the rest. There was never, at the time, any thought or suggestion of one boy being uniquely gifted.

"They seemed to develop together," Mr White reports. "One suggested this, another that, and each more or less incorporated in his work the discoveries of the whole."

Soon word of the remarkable work being produced at Carrolup

began to spread round. Visiting inspectors reported themselves increasingly impressed, and often took pictures away with them to show to other school teachers. The work, however, was received with some scepticism outside. Few believed that it was unassisted, and if convinced of this would never have it that Mr or Mrs White was not gifted artistically.

Newspaper articles now began to appear about the children's pictures, and Mr White was urged to bring some of his pupils and their work to Perth. An exhibition was arranged in a gallery at Boans, a big store in the centre of the city, and interested people undertook to board the boys.

Very smart in new safari suits made by the devoted and capable Mrs White, they attracted attention as they walked through the streets of the city, where the sight of a single aboriginal is now rare enough and that of a group of neat, well-brushed, and bright-faced young darkies was unique. It was a new and wonderful experience to the bush children. Used, in country towns, to being shunned and rebuffed, they could at first register no more than startled surprise when escorted round town by friendly newspapermen, when passers-by stopped them with friendly smiles and they heard themselves spoken of on all sides.

"Look! There go the young Abo artists!"

Strangers stopped them with gifts of sweets and fruit, and some—to Mr White's embarrassment—even money. It was explained that the boys might have the fruit and sweets, but money they must decline. Perhaps, however, these kind people might like to see the children's work and buy a small example for a few shillings, which would be used towards providing further materials.

By the time they reached the big store at which they were to display their skill they had gathered a large following. Solemnly eating loquats presented them by an admirer at the door, they proceeded to the lift. Here in an effort to rid themselves of the embarrassment before arriving at the gallery, they dropped the stones on the floor.

"You can't do that there here!" the lift attendant admonished them. "You're not in the bush now, you know."

The boys, overcome with nervousness and shame, scrambled apologetically about, gathering up and pocketing the offending seeds.

"Sorry, sir! We didn't know!"

The attendant was impressed, for like many townies he had never encountered aborigines before.

"Where did you learn the lingo?"

"It grew on us, sir!"

Before the exhibition week was over he had become their firm friend and protector, allowing them endless rides and patiently explained the mechanism of the lift.

"They're the Indian cricketers," he one day mischievously informed an inquiring passenger. All eyes were turned on the abashed boys. Claude Kelly evidently felt it unfair to lead these kindly city Wadjelars into so serious a misapprehension.

"Aw—we're not the Indian cricketers. We're only a bunch of Noongars from Carrolup!"

However pleased they may have been at the praise and interest aroused by their work, they did not see themselves as anything other than a group of humble natives, to whom white people, according to their unpredictable whims, chose to be kindly, hostile, or merely indifferent.

During this visit the boys made a tour of inspection of the Perth Museum and Art Gallery. They were intrigued to discover a wonderful collection of native weapons and to realize that they had not always portrayed these accurately in their pictures. They took careful note of detail and did not repeat the mistakes. The ochre paintings of their native forbears, here seen by them for the first time, they considered poor workmanship, though interesting enough and not without humour, but the art of the European Moderns they would not entertain at all. Only Parnell Dempster, a kindly and tolerant lad, thought they should not be dismissed without a word of encouragement.

"Some nice colour there," he admitted, head on one side, indicating the print of a Seurat. "Leave him alone! That fellow might come good by and by!"

The pictures were next exhibited publicly at a school of instruction for a hundred teachers in the south-western town of Albany. Nothing among the work displayed approached that of Carrolup for originality, colour, and sheer drawing ability.

Mr White, who had brought the work himself, was naturally anxious to know how it would be received, and he was nonplussed to hear it said that the work was "too good to be true," that it was asking too much of the public to accept this as unassisted child art. In vain Mr White protested on behalf of his pupils. It was at last Mr Crabbe, the education inspector, who suggested Mr White's returning to Carrolup for four or five of his pupils to give a personal demonstration of their skill. Next day, spruced up for their entry into the big town, the children filed into the hall with their teacher. Tables, paper, and other materials were promptly provided, and the sceptical throng gathered round.

Without hesitation, and as though oblivious to the curious audience, the children bent over their task. Soon each had finished a picture, different in subject and arrangement, but similar in style to those on exhibition. Kangaroos bounded across brown summer landscapes, up the green hillsides of winter, through fire-charred trees stark against the verdant bush. Moonlight glowed on brimming swamps between the white trunks of the flooded gums. Sunsets blazed behind the darkened silhouettes of slender jam-trees. Painted black men danced round corroboree fires or stalked their prey through lonely valleys. Mr White added these pictures to those on the wall.

"All right, boys! Home now!"

They departed in an orderly procession, leaving behind a surprised and thoughtful gathering.

CHAPTER NINE

THE WHIM OF THE WADJELARS

For a while the children's extraordinary work, the unconcern with which they continued to sketch under the curious eyes of onlookers, their unspoilt and courteous behaviour, was on every one's lips. After the children returned to Carrolup a certain amount of newspaper controversy went on as to whether they should be given art-lessons or left to their own devices.

As to what the future held for their pupils Mr and Mrs White had no theories. They only knew that through their art-work life had been made worth while for the children in their charge and an approach had been made to other educational subjects. They felt that if the work did no more than draw attention to the need for general improvement of conditions at Carrolup it would have played a valuable part.

It was later reported to headquarters that the children were not improved by so much notice and publicity, though it is doubtful that it touched them very closely. They heard that people admired their work but, knowing nothing of the struggle of white artists for recognition and the value attached to it, it did not seem to them of any great significance. They were pleased to be able to please—an age-old aboriginal trait. They had, of course, no measuring stick of quality, no means of weighing values. Their egos could be as quickly deflated as inflated, and Mr White had a delicate task in keeping them to a middle course.

The publicity, however, was short-lived, and the little school continued as before. Mr White, in consultation with the Department and with various inspectors who had watched over the children's progress, realized the necessity of helping the youngsters to take their place in the world of white people. They must be taught to mingle and be brought to understand the meaning of such things as team-work and sportsmanship. Art must not be allowed to assume unpractical proportions or to keep them from health-giving activities and sports. Football, running, jumping, and other forms of physical development were given prominence in the curriculum, and in due course co-operative headmasters of other state schools invited the Carrolup boys to competitive sports meetings.

A crowd of happy boys came again to the city, with kangaroos emblazoned in bright yellow on their football jerseys. Again the children awakened public interest. None of the town teams stood much chance against these thin, though wiry, children from the bush. Their spindly native legs were designed for speed, their spare frames for endurance.

"Abo Team amazes City," "Bush Boys Victorious!" ran the headlines. "Give them wings and they'd fly," one paper reported. Big crowds roared with enthusiasm at their nimbleness, and applauded with spontaneous delight when Tommy Dawson, the baby of the Carrolup team, suddenly left the game, pulled off his boots, threw them at the feet of his teacher, and hastened back to the fray!

People with whom the children were boarded were delighted with their behaviour and good manners, and plans were made for a summer holiday at the seaside for both girls and boys during the Christmas recess, while Mr and Mrs White were on holiday. Some of the youngsters were boarded with private families and behaved most creditably. Others were housed in a Government building, which, like any crowd of high-spirited and inadequately supervised children, they appear to have lightheartedly wrecked.

The storm of criticism was now as loud as the previous words of praise. The Carrolup children had reverted to type! The youngsters returned home somewhat under a cloud. The whim of the Wadjelars had turned against them. But it made little difference whether or not they basked in the favour of the white community. Their joy lay increasingly in their work, their nature paintings, and their handicrafts.

Over the period of three and a half years since Mr and Mrs White took over charge of the school certain changes had occurred. In 1948 the Government, conscious of the increase of the coloured people and of the need of a reformed policy for them, appointed a special magistrate to survey the entire position. In the course of his investigation Mr F. E. Bateman visited all native institutions and places of native employment throughout the state, reported fully on each, and made certain recommendations. Of Carrolup, one of about thirty native institutions, he wrote:

> The population, mainly mixed bloods, was at this time 163, including 103 children. . . . The school is staffed by Mr and Mrs White, both qualified teachers. . . . The teaching here has attained a standard not seen elsewhere in the native schools and is largely due to the excellent methods adopted by Mr White. About half a dozen children are in the sixth standard, and I understand that their work is equivalent to that of white pupils in the same class in the state schools. The art-work, however, is remarkable, being very much advanced on white standards. No vocational training unfortunately is provided on the settlement, and it is a matter of regret that the good work Mr and Mrs White are doing among the children is largely wasted because of the undesirable associations entered into by the children after school hours.

The Department realized that many things needed attention at Carrolup and that older natives, mostly sent on criminal charges, were the worst possible influence on young people. Most of the adult natives were accordingly transferred to Moore River Settlement. After that things proceeded much as before, the year fairly regularly punctuated with the arrival and departure of staff-members. Only an occasional short burst of publicity reminded people of the child artists. A Carrolup boy won a state-wide painting competition, and a Perth artist, Beatrice Darbyshire, who had been interested in their work since their first exhibition, arranged an exhibition in Sydney. Here again they created lively interest and enthusiasm and some speculation as to their future, but Sydney is far from Perth, remote indeed from so tiny a settlement as Carrolup.

Many interested and kindly people would have helped with money or time, but all avenues of approach seemed to lead to a dead end—back at Carrolup. The matter was in the hands of the Department and was receiving 'all due consideration.'

Only a few faithful friends worried consistently as to what the future really held for the children whose progress they had watched so carefully. Among these were Mr G. S. Crabbe (a school inspector), Mr J. P. Stokes (a headmaster), and a few journalists, who endeavoured to sustain interest in the Carrolup children's work. Muriel Weike, writing in the Perth journal *Milady* in July 1949, four years after Mr and Mrs White first came to Carrolup, revived the story and reproduced in colour examples of the work. It was this story and the accompanying pictures which first attracted Mrs Rutter's attention to the existence of the young artists.

CHAPTER TEN

CARROLUP COMES TO LONDON

AND still, after pursuing various avenues of inquiry, the task seemed simple enough. Here was a group of gifted children in need of recognition and an opportunity of attaining a place in the community. If nothing were done for them they would leave school at fourteen years of age and drift about the countryside, taking employment here and there in timber-mills, or as farm labourers. Without incentive to save and make good they would not apply for citizen rights. Their earnings would be spent on sly grog and gambling, and as likely as not they would end back in the settlements from which they started life. The girls would have even less chance. Most of them would be mothers by the time they were sixteen or seventeen, some even before. For them life offered little outside the settlements, although many would take employment as domestics on farms, drifting from job to job, perhaps trying at last to gather their families together in a 'home' made from pieces of rusty scrap-iron and such odds and ends as could be salvaged from the rubbish heaps.

This was what Mr White meant when he sadly informed the visitor that he feared there was little future for his pupils. Some of his children were already almost of school-leaving age and were growing restless to be out in the world earning money and 'knocking about,' and he knew that the confidence they now had in themselves stood little chance of surviving the temptations and rebuffs that were the native's lot.

If this were the case it seemed only reasonable that the boys should be kept at school under the guidance of Mr and Mrs White until sixteen years of age. In these two years they could be given every opportunity to develop their art-work and handicrafts and to be taught such trades as would render them useful and valued members of the community. Children of exceptional promise might be permitted to carry their artistic or technical training further—to be given, in short, the advantages to which talented white children are entitled.

Mrs Rutter was confident that once the children's work was made widely known and their ability recognized other difficulties would be solved. Their potential value as citizens would be realized and their path cleared of obstacles that had debarred previous generations from making any headway in the community.

The Minister for Native Affairs, when approached on the subject, agreed warmly that something should be done to further the education of the children, and he suggested a round table conference with various officials concerned on Mrs Rutter's return from other Australasian capitals.

With her precious pictures mounted on white cardboard and covered with cellophane, Mrs Rutter set out upon her journey. Side by side with the founding of clubs in various capitals she advertised and exhibited the work of the children of Carrolup. In Adelaide, Melbourne, and Sydney, in the capitals of Tasmania and New Zealand, she worked tirelessly on behalf of her protégés. Newspapers and magazines published articles and reproduced examples of the work, wireless stations devoted time to interviewing Mrs Rutter and broadcasting descriptions of the children's work. Public interest and sympathy was aroused, and in certain capitals spontaneous subscriptions enabled Mrs Rutter to return to the children with the best available materials—soft French pastels, good oil- and water-colours. So many orders had been obtained for examples of the Carrolup work that her dream of a self-supporting art-centre for gifted native children seemed now a practical proposition.

Meanwhile the Department in the West had been giving Carrolup its serious consideration. Now that the settlement had ceased to be just another impossible native reserve and had become the focal point of so much publicity it was obvious that money must be found for improvements, and something in the nature of a progressive policy embarked upon. Now that the five-o'clock curfew had been lifted and a more humane attitude prevailed it seemed that if there had not yet been any trouble between the growing boys and girls there assuredly soon would be. It seemed wisest to declare Carrolup a boys' town and remove the girls to various missions.

Past Administrations had fought the missions on many issues, even declaring it to be their policy to replace them in time by Government-run reserves and settlements, but the administrative pendulum had swung again. If the missions had, for various reasons, achieved little towards establishing the native in the outside community, the Government institutions had assuredly achieved nothing. The Department had proved itself a well-intentioned, but too overburdened, parent, and if it had in the past been more alive than missions to the need for progressive policy it had been unable to implement its schemes. It was increasingly clear that the casual Government recruit was no match for the zeal and devotion of the missionary, approaching his work as a vocation. Many religious institutions seemed now aware that the day of simple evangelism and attempts to uplift was past and were turning their attention to improved educational and vocational training. Departmental policy would therefore now tend towards the closing of Government settlements and the provision of better facilities for missions. Well-run missions are known to handle domestic problems more efficiently than Government-run institutions, and if this policy is coupled with a plan to co-operate with the Education Department for the provision of trained teachers it should show results.

In the meantime, however, conditions at Carrolup must be at least to some extent improved. Before Mrs Rutter's return a new superintendent, with organizing experience in Papua, was appointed to Carrolup and was able to join in the round-table conference, which included the Commissioner for Native Affairs, Mr and Mrs White, and Mrs Gordon Hack, who had accompanied Mrs Rutter to the Native Settlement. Every one seemed in agreement as to future plans. All wished the best for the children, and the way to their establishment in the community was clearly seen. A trust fund, into which was paid the money collected by Mrs Rutter from sales of the work, was started on behalf of the young artists. The Department had it in mind to turn Carrolup into a technical training centre, and it seemed well within the range of possibility that a properly equipped art school be established under the direction of Mr White.

Certainly the Department would see to it that boys of promise were not sent out to work as farm labourers and timber-cutters. They would be given every possible opportunity. Already one Carrolup boy, Barry Loo, who had attained school-leaving age, had been brought to Perth and put to work in the Department as an office-boy. Very soon others would be sent for to join him. Barry, looking spruce and smart in his city clothes, was called in to prove the point.

Mrs Rutter was disappointed to hear that the girls, whose designs had created so much interest and commendation, had left Carrolup just as conditions were about to be improved. She agreed, however, that if the move was for their ultimate benefit the Department had no doubt acted wisely.

After the meeting, and on her way to Carrolup for her second and more lengthy visit, she was able to visit some of the girls in their new home, the mission at Wandering Brook, run by Catholic nuns. Here was a very different picture from the Government settlement at Carrolup. The little girls were neat and clean, their dormitories and classrooms spotless and well-equipped. They were happy and undoubtedly well cared for. Their school-work appeared to be average and they had produced some fine embroidery, but artistically they could show nothing of note—a flower-pot, a butterfly, a lighted candle.

"What of the work you did at Carrolup?" Mrs Rutter asked. But already they seemed to have forgotten.

At Carrolup Mrs Rutter, after a rousing welcome from the boys, had the joy of distributing the gifts of paints and crayons and telling the children how greatly their work had been appreciated throughout the country. She was able to show them newspaper photographs of people gathering to admire their work when hung on exhibition in the big capital cities.

The boys, sucking the sweets their champion had brought them, smiled happily and went off to their midday meal. When they reassembled Mr White suggested to them that he was sure they would each like to do a little picture with their new colours for Mrs Rutter to take home to her family and friends.

No direction was given as to subject. The boys nodded their heads, bent over their desks, and with intense concentration set to work. Although Mrs Rutter and her friend walked behind the boys at work, not a head was raised until a finished picture was presented—each a beautiful study in art, executed within two hours!

Returning each night to Katanning, Mrs Rutter spent three days with the children and their teachers, introducing Parnell Dempster to the medium of oil-painting, showing him how to mix his colours on a palette, making plans for the future, and gathering together a wide selection of pictures, many to dispatch in fulfilment of orders collected on her tour, over a hundred others to exhibit abroad.

She promised the children to do all in her power to make their work known throughout the world and through it assist them to citizenship. The children cheered her lustily. It seemed to them then that the troubles of their people were over. They would show the way to a new era for all the wandering and derelict families of the Great Southern. Mr and Mrs White were also optimistic, for with local authorities in apparently happy agreement there seemed little to prevent the fulfilment of their most cherished dreams.

Back in England Mrs Rutter lost no time in commencing her campaign for the children of Carrolup. She immediately published a pamphlet entitled *Little Black Fingers*, giving, along with the reproduction of some of the pictures, an outline of the children's story. This served both as a catalogue and a means of furthering publicity while awaiting the appointed exhibition date.

The pictures were first exhibited abroad at the Art Gallery in Apeldoorn, Holland, where an extremely art-conscious public, curators of larger galleries, school-children, and their teachers expressed themselves amazed and charmed by the children's work.

The London opening, in the Hall of India and Pakistan, at the Over-seas League, coincided with the social occasion of New Members' night, July 28, 1950, exactly one year after Mrs Rutter's first introduction to aboriginal art and her first visit to a native settlement. A distinguished and colourful gathering from many countries was deeply impressed by the quality and freshness of the work of these Australian bush children. Many declared the exhibition incredible. Paper after paper took up the story of Carrolup. *The Times Educational Supplement*, *The Daily Express*, *The Daily Graphic*, *The Illustrated London News*, *The Teachers' World*, *Studio*, and a score of other publications reproduced pictures with descriptions and speculative articles. "Little Black Fingers create Sensation!" "Is this Mediumship?" "Easy-money Racket or Real Art?" "Children's Art thrills London." "Scribbling by Nature Boys startles London Artists." "Is this Primitive Art?" "Can Your Child draw like This?" These are only a few of the headlines chosen at random.

Educationists, psychologists, anthropologists—all had their say, all endeavouring to solve the mystery of this new and unexpected form of child art. The following extract from an article by Mr Horace Shipp in *The Teachers' World* of February 7, 1951, after an exhibition earlier that month at Foyle's Gallery, Charing

Cross Road, London, will suffice to give the trend of more thoughtful opinion:

> The typical result we reproduce on our centre pages, but we cannot reproduce the brilliance, the harmony of colour, nor the abundance of this work. No teacher, no educationalist interested in art should miss this exhibition. . . . Both formal and atmospheric perspective are perfectly observed and depicted. In fact, this is absolutely the art of things seen, an art of visual memory with something of the miracle of cavemen's art. . . .
>
> These children saw in perspective. The far trees *looked* smaller than the near ones, the river *looked* narrow in the distance, the colours of remote things appeared less bright than those near. So they put them down and, more marvellous still, they stored them precisely in their minds, so that the boys sit at their desks and from their visual memory recreate these things without difficulty.
>
> The important fact is that their copy was nature. Or, if mutual imitation came into it the conception was based on nature . . . and—this is a point of utmost importance on our own educational methods—their school walls would not be covered with examples of distortion, crudity, and naive "child art," nor would they be taken to exhibitions showing hundreds of such works. . . . This art of the Bushman children of Carrolup poses a score of problems of education, psychology, of anthropology, of civilization itself. Not least it challenges in certain respects the fashionable theories of our own art education with their distrust of naturalist vision and their pompous epigrams about children not painting what they see.
>
> True it may demonstrate the wisdom of 'leaving alone.' But suppose a child left alone in one of our advanced art rooms happens to have a genius of this kind, would it receive the approbation of the ultra-modern theorists and the pontiffs of the Society of Art Education? Or be discouraged as a mere copyist heading straight for the Royal Academy?[1]

[1] Quoted by courtesy of the author and the Editor of *The Teachers' World.*

CHAPTER ELEVEN

ART AND THE ABORIGINAL

In Australia too discussions had arisen regarding the Carrolup art. Many were quite uncritically surprised and enchanted by the children's work. Others expressed scepticism as to its merits, a doubt arising not from prejudice so much as from the vision splendid of a Great Australian Art Form. The familiar cry went up: "But this is not aboriginal art! Why were they not *left alone*?"

Ever since the aborigines first showed themselves to possess artistic facility they have been looked to to effect a vague culture fusion—an art at once new and old, vital and significant. It is argued that many promising native artists have been ruined by interference and 'help,' that they were better left to their own devices, not encouraged to express themselves in the white man's idiom or with the white man's materials. Only then, it is said, could we hope for the development of a true Australian art.

But, alas, the idiom of the old men is not that of this generation of natives—with the exception of a few isolated and more or less untouched people in remote corners of the far North who continue to reproduce careful replicas of time-honoured formulas. The sky heroes that were the inspiration of the old artists mean nothing to the black Australians of to-day. To them, the old symbols are as quaint and even mysterious as they are to us.

"Black-fellow humbug!" the modern native remarks, with a disparaging gesture towards a rock-face resplendent with stylized god-men and culture heroes of the time long past that were to his ancestors the mainspring of life and religious inspiration. The modern aboriginal, in fact, regards the art of his forefathers rather as a snake regards its cast-off skin. He has grown out of it, and it is to him of no further use or interest. Has not the missionary made it clear that the ancient gods were at best figments of savage superstition, at worst devil-spirits of darkness and corruption, that his old beliefs and customs must be discarded if he is to find salvation? There were idealists who believed that the aborigines might well keep the best of their own culture, blending it with the best of ours; but the faith of the old people was *a way of life and thought* not to be divided into component parts —this good, that bad. It was an intricate mosaic of meaning only in its entirety.

If the aboriginal develops artistically it hardly seems likely that his work will be a *further development* of his own art or even a new and interesting culture fusion or interpretation of his old and new ways of life. Just as the scientist may pick up the cast skin as a thing of meaning to him, so it is the scientist and later the white artist who has picked up the cast-off art of the aboriginal. It is the white artist, delighting in aboriginal design, often attracted also to the philosophy as reflected in the work, who effects the fusion of cultures we would look for from the native. It is possible that some aboriginal may in time be sufficiently influenced by the work of white artists who have already introduced an element of aboriginal art to do so likewise, though the inspiration will hardly arise until he has come round full cycle to look upon the religious symbols of his past with the eyes of a white man.

When tribal life began to break down in Australia any possibility of leaving the aboriginal alone artistically no longer existed. Whether he liked it or not he was swept along, albeit at his own more leisurely pace, on the same currents and tides of social change and conflict as ourselves. It was not possible to fix his artistic development in the fossil-bed of a totemic past. He was alive and he was curious. He was bored with the idea of painting ancient symbols and patterns with grey ash, charcoal, white clay, and yellow ochre. He liked colours, and he wanted to use as many as he could lay hands to. He quickly grasped the idea of realistic expression—of drawing as one *saw*, not as one *knew*. When the old tribal artists drew animals they portrayed the intestines as well as the outer forms because they *knew* they were there, but this, the native was quick to decide, was also "black-fellow humbug."

To 'leave the native artist alone' is not as simple as it sounds, because he is influenced by everything he sees in his new environment. He must go about with his eyes closed if he is nowhere to encounter any of the white man's forbidden pictures. They stare at him from every newspaper, every jam-label, every hoarding. From the point of view of influence he is lost when once he discards his woven-hair girdle for a pair of trousers.

"Protect him, then, from falling into the *wrong hands*!" the idealist protests, and here indeed we are posed with a problem, for who is to be the mentor of the 'right' and the 'wrong' hands? Who is to decide whether he be allowed to paint in the manner of a Gauguin or a Constable, a Picasso or an Augustus John?

The discovery of artistic facility in the aborigines is so recent that we are as yet unable to see it in any perspective. We are still rather in the stage of happy surprise with which one watches human activities on the parts of circus animals.

It is not so many years since the name of Albert Namatjira was unknown beyond the confines of the Central Australian mission at Hermansberg. Now there can hardly be an Australian who does not know of his work. For all the moderns' protest against the influences under which he fell, for all they may disparage the conventional nature of his water-colour technique, he has, besides opening the eyes of the world to the wild beauty of his country, bringing the wonder of Australia's 'red heart' to brighten the walls of city homes, he has probably done more, through his work, than any other individual to bring about a change of heart and attitude towards his people.

If the artist Rex Battarbee, fearful of influencing a possible protégé, had studiously refrained from giving him a box of water-colours and a few simple instructions in their use, had zealously hidden from him any works from his own brush, we would assuredly never have heard of Namatjira or any of the younger, possibly more vigorous Aranda[1] artists who were in turn helped by him and encouraged by his success.

There must be dozens of potential native artists who have been 'left alone,' but have produced nothing that has come to our notice. It would seem that this extraordinary artistic facility, so rare in our society, perhaps so overlaid with self-consciousness as to be almost lost, is more or less common to the aboriginal. Even though few of the Carrolup children were full-bloods, there is no doubt that any æsthetic sense they possess comes rather from their proud, gentle, aboriginal ancestors, with their sense of mysticism and everlasting things, than from the feckless white men who fathered and abandoned the children of their black mothers and grandmothers. Left alone, or given perhaps into the hands of some one less patient and understanding than Mr and Mrs White, there is also little doubt that the Carrolup children would never have achieved any form of expression at all—artistic

[1] Or Arunta, the big Central Australian tribe.

A Ramble in the Bush

These drawings, describing a ramble in the bush, are executed in Nature's colours in crayon. They are from Revel Cooper's school-book in his last term.

THE CARDAR

This is another page from Revel Cooper's school-book. Note the border of aboriginal implements, so often used by these artists to surround their pictures. The cardar is a variety of lizard.

or otherwise. In subsequent discussions this vital factor appears to have been overlooked.

As with Namatjira, the work must be considered also from the point of view of its byproducts, the social questions it arouses and the social changes it may effect. No doubt suggestions that these children may have developed more interestingly if left alone are surely made in ignorance of their story, as are also the regrets expressed that this is not 'aboriginal art.' The work is that of children of aboriginal blood who know as little of the art-forms of their forefathers as they do of the moderns, or, for that matter of any artists of our own society. They were no more or less influenced than any of their kind with eyes to see and ears to hear in a white man's world. But what they produced was something spontaneous and unique of itself. Whether the work will be a thing of lasting interest, 'significant' in the light of later years, only time can tell.

It can only be said that Australia has not seen the like of this work before, and, despite the fact that so many people of aboriginal blood are artistically inclined, it is doubtful whether the phenomenon of Carrolup—an unusual combination of circumstances and a vital teacher-pupil relationship—will ever occur again.

CHAPTER TWELVE

LETTERS FROM CARROLUP

FROM London Mrs Rutter wrote to the Department for Native Affairs in Perth and the children at Carrolup telling of the tremendous success of the exhibitions. She spoke of the formation of a London council to further the interests of the young artists abroad, and she sent bulky packets of cuttings from English newspapers. The children and their teachers were greatly encouraged by the news and were full of optimism for the future.

The boys, in response to her request for something about themselves and their backgrounds, poured out their hearts in neat little letters decorated with crayon sketches of Carrolup landscape and the inevitable kangaroos. Extracts from these are quoted as written.

"Because you are gone thats no need for us not writing to you," thirteen-year-old Laurie Champion began.

> I wish I were you when you were on your long journey across the wide sea. . . . Now Mrs Rutter you will be very interesting to know that he will be doing metal work and my job is now to get the cows in and get them milked before sunrise.

Barry Loo wrote responsibly from the Department in Perth:

> I greatly appreciate your very kind letter you wrote to me regarding art work.
>
> First and foremost I would like to tell you my story of art and about the illustrated nature study lessons.
>
> In school we used to have one nature study lesson a week, the afternoon before the day, Mr White used to take us for a ramble in the bush and in that way we found and learnt the rare things of nature. The next day we would illustrate everything we saw on the ramble.
>
> Mr White would later tell us to take an individual animal and illustrate everything we could about it and in this way we learnt to draw animals in all positions.

How we, us boys come to do such beautiful art work of scenic and bush scenes is that we spent all our precious play hours at school and weekends doing this work and three years of this took our art work up to where it is today, and I say all honours are on Mr White who gave us that opportunity to improve our work. . . .

I remain,

Yours Respectfully forever,

BARRY ALBERT LOO

Reynold Hart, with characteristic earnestness, had set himself the task of an autobiographical outline.

I am going to tell you of the past years of my life. I came to Carrolup when I was four years of age, my father was living at Collie at this time. . . .

When I arrived at Carrolup there were many other boys and girls there. The first two or three months I was a bit worried for my parents, it wasn't long after that I began to settle down and liked my new home.

I was put in a big dormitary where I was given a bed to sleep in. At that time I was treated very cruelly.

Two years after that I was put into school. I soon picked up my lessons and was beginning to like my school work. . . .

When I became seven, our school was closed down for two years. That was the time we missed most of our school work. Then two teachers came here. One was Mrs Elliot and the other lady was Mrs Blonde.

The first week of school I was put right back in my work. I had to make a fresh start.

After Mrs Elliot went, Mr White came. The first year he came here he found all the school children running round in the bush, looking like savages. Then he started to learn us some music. He had a flute which he used to play for us in school Then when he saw we were keen on music he started to learn us a few songs. The first song he learnt us was Three Pigs. It wasn't long before he had learnt us a big list of songs.

Then he picked a batch of boys to do some drawings. He saw then that we had some talent, we practised on brown paper night after night for about two years and our drawing started to win the respect of the white people. That was the year we had an exhibition of Art in Perth.

The native children in the past wasn't given a chance to learn, but since Mr White took over the teaching at Carrolup we are now getting people to respect us and our drawings.

Now I am little over fourteen I am starting to see new changes happening with us. Last year we went down to Perth to play a football match with the boys from Thomas Street School.

Before Mr White came to Carrolup nobody ever heard the name of Carrolup, but now it is nearly known all over the world. So now I am getting older I would like to take my place in this world amongst other people and be respected as a decent citizen of Australia.

I sometimes feel I'd like to work as a Commercial Artist or have a sheep farm of my own.

Other letters contained scattered pieces of information, little glimpses of the various children's lives and characters.

Now I am going to tell you how I came here, when I was home I had two big sisters up here and they kept running away and they brought us back and that is why I am up here now.

Last Saturday the white boys came and play us cricket and we won them. . . . We are going to be Scout boys. I made a boat out of a pinetree bark.

Simpson Kelly, although one of the most prolific young artists, wrote exclusively of sport:

The other day, we went to a sports other side of Kojonup. We didn't know where it was, but we were only to glad to go. Soon as we jumped off the truck the man who runs the sports, said that he would like to have some boys in the race. Parnell and Reynold said that they would have a race up against the champion runner of Muraderup. So they had a race. Parnell was the first and Reynold came second.

Philip Jackson, another artist, clearly indicated that his ambitions did not lie in artistic channels:

Every time the truck goes for water I sit in front watching how the man drive. I go for the cows and milk them. They only give three buckets because most of them are dry.

My ambition is to drive the big truck of wheat carting it to Perth.

Thirteen-year-old Ross Jones wrote briefly and to the point:

I was born in Wagin . . . and then my mother took me to the Gnowerangerup Mission.

Then my mother brought me to Carrolup, in 1940. I was three years old.

> I went to school at the age of seven. That was when we wasn't educated properly. Now we are. . . .
> I dont know anything of my farther.

Jimmy Dabb indicated that he had crammed a great deal of variety into his ten years.

> I came from Moore River and we went from Mogumber to Perth. And when I was in Perth we went for a ride in a boat out in the sea. And then we went to sea the zoo. In school I like drawing. On Friday morning we went to see the sports. Parnell and Rennel and two white men were racing. Parnell and Rennel won the race. Well Mrs Rutter if you want to know my age here it is age ten.

Cliff Ryder, after relating how he had won the manual training prize in the Katanning district and how Mr White said he was "proving" with his drawing, confessed that he too would like to be a truck-driver taking wheat to Perth.

John Cuttabit had the traditional small boy's longing to become an engine-driver. In fact, the letters indicate that very few of the children thought of art as a career, though many referred to it as having won them the respect of the white people.

Parnell Dempster, never outstandingly articulate, wrote briefly: "Now I am fourteen years old. I would like to be something good. I don't like camp life."

Later letters indicated that changes were afoot at the settlement: "Did you know that our dormitories have had another room put on them and that they have been painted. They are much better now." "Have you heard that Parnell went to work in Perth?" But as time went on further correspondence from the children, endeavouring to explain why the promised pictures were not forthcoming, indicated that all was not proceeding to plan.

Inquiries at headquarters elicited the information that owing to the many difficulties involved in maintaining such an institution the school at Carrolup was to be closed!

CHAPTER THIRTEEN

DEPARTMENTAL DILEMMA

THE Department for Native Affairs had been called upon in the past to cope with many complex problems of *degeneration*, but here was a completely new and bewildering problem of *regeneration*, to which no clause in the 'Act' offered as much as a clue. After so many years of struggle and disappointment with its coloured people it was quite unprepared to meet the challenge of a group of promising boys. The call was obviously for a well-organized vocational training centre to which the school children could graduate but there was no such thing in the state outside one or two progressive missions, and these were somewhat under subsidized and still in the experimental stage.

For so long the best-intentioned people had declared the task of getting anywhere with these people a thankless and impossible one. This was regrettable, but could be understood and dealt with according to precedent, by the constant replacement of inexperienced and mostly unsuitable staff, but a man who had found the task both gratifying and possible, who had exercised an extraordinary influence and produced totally unlooked-for results, had become something of an embarrassment.

The situation now presented a completely new array of teasing questions. What, for instance, *was* the long and short of this art question that now tended to overshadow all other aspects of native welfare? Were these children really interested in art for art's sake, or was it no more than a welcome diversion from the tedium of school-work? Was it advisable to encourage them to become artists? Surely artists in our own society were difficult enough to cope with and had a hard enough struggle to make ends meet! How *good* was the boy's work anyway? Was it good *of itself* or was it to be regarded as a promise of things to come? If the latter, how would they best develop? Kept at school under the encouragement of Mr White? Left alone to take their chance in the world with other would-be artists, to develop in their own time and at their own pace? Sent to technical colleges to study commercial art? Taught trades and encouraged to pursue their art-work as a hobby?

Admittedly the children's work had startled the public, but would the public go on being startled, or even interested, if the pictures kept pouring out at great pace and with no marked improvement? Most natives were willing to mass-produce on promise of reward, sacrificing quality and inspiration to quantity. One saw on the Transcontinental Railway Line the result of a tourist trade in 'sacred emblems' and native weapons. One had also seen the results of group-art in Central Australia.

Also, what was to be done with the steadily increasing trust fund from sales of pictures? In equipping a proper art-school it would be a drop in the ocean. On the other hand, it was more than was required for the provision of materials.

The possibility of erecting a modern studio at Carrolup and allowing the more talented boys to remain there for a while after leaving school had admittedly been considered. The art question, however, became more vexed and involved with the passage of every week. The Department did not lack advice from various sources, but the suggestions were of so contradictory a nature as to confuse an already complicated issue. A harassed Commissioner, subjected to a shower of letters and deputations, to the backwash of what had now become a highly charged conflict of personalities, ideas, and ideals, and at the same time watching the expense of reorganizing Carrolup threatening to overbalance the Departmental budget, was in a quandary. Carrolup was, after all, only one of the Department's many responsibilities, and the amount of time and correspondence it was now demanding seemed out of all proportion to its importance.

The situation had reached a stage when an ever-widening number of interested persons and parties were outspokenly suspecting each other's motives and bandying about the witch-word 'exploitation.' Rather belatedly questions arose as to whether the pictures and their reproduction rights belonged to the young artists, their parents (if any), the Department of Education, or the Department of Native Affairs. Now that the art-work that had made Carrolup famous had been taken from the walls and scattered to the four winds it was seen that it might have been more appropriately used in decorating departmental offices! The Department wanted most earnestly to be proud of its charges, to have something to show as a result of its work for the coloured people, and now the only tangible result of years of effort had disappeared. Certainly the pictures had not been taken without permission. It had appeared at the time that there would be plenty more where these came from, but now that it seemed advisable to dampen the enthusiasm for art at Carrolup it was a different matter.

It seemed in the eyes of the Department that an artistic education had clearly exercised no stabilizing effect on the Carrolup children. The three boys brought to the city had proved a disappointment. Parnell Dempster had joined Barry Loo as an office boy, while Reynold Hart had been apprenticed as a painter at the Public Works. All three were encouraged to attend night classes in Commercial Art at the Technical school, but it was evidently one thing to draw trees and kangaroos under the kindly eye of Mr White, quite another to be put to lettering with precision instruments! In the office the boys became tired, not so much from overwork as from lack of it. The job had been made for them and they knew it, knew too, no doubt, that they were not of any real importance there. They had learned to work hard and diligently at tasks that held their interest and stimulated their creative sense. Office work, running messages, waiting about for the odd job, though novel for a time, quickly palled. Parnell wrote homesick little letters irrelevantly decorated with nostalgic pictures of Carrolup country and bounding kangaroos—hardly, a disappointed Department pointed out, the work of the average sixth-standard schoolboy. Reynold Hart appeared to be working happily and was popular with his workmates, but soon he too grew homesick. Mrs Rutter had suggested Reynold Hart should be put to painting a mural round the hospital wards rather than painting the woodwork of doors and windows of the hospital, This would have been a lasting testimony to the boy's wonderful gift, and, still more important, a means of health-giving joy to the patients. All three became restless and unhappy in their places of residence, and one by one asked leave to go off and visit their people. Permission was granted and none of the three returned.

A disillusioned entry in official files suggested that they evidently preferred the old vagabond conditions of native camp-life to the good accommodation and opportunities provided them in the city. But the Department's attitude towards the boys had been kindly and paternal. Many efforts had been made to help them feel happy and at home, and their lack of response was hurtful and disappointing. The experiment, however, was not fruitless. It indicated that it is one thing to expect nothing of a people, to dismiss it as entirely unemployable, and another thing to expect too much too soon. Because the native is no longer to be relegated to the rubbish heap it is perhaps too sudden a swing of the pendulum to put him automatically into the category of the white-collar worker, even entertaining some hopes of his attaining professional standing. After all, the most consistent of Mr White's pupils had had no more than three to four years' regular schooling, and the effects of their early environment were not to be forgotten over-night. Few white boys of the same schooling would be likely to prove themselves up-and-coming office-workers, keen to improve themselves by attending evening classes.

By no means lacking in intelligence or ambition, these boys would no doubt have excelled at some form of artisanship. To work with their hands had always been their keenest joy, the source of any satisfaction and confidence they had ever known. Reynold Hart would no doubt have done well enough in the public works but for the need of companionship of his own kind. The Department realized this and set to work on plans for a boys' hostel for promising youngsters wishing to be trained in various trades. A place of the kind for girls had already been established in a good suburb, and after strenuous opposition and outcry from the white residents was proving successful.

Meanwhile at Carrolup improvements were under way. The whole place was reorganized, painted, scrubbed, disinfected, the diet improved, staff quarters brought up to standard. The superintendent felt that it must be a case of first things first. He was conscientious and had ideas for raising the boys' general social standard. The art question seemed rather beside the point, an unnecessary complication. The long and patient work of Mr and Mrs White in building up the children's confidence and leading them, through their natural interests, to a wide range of school subjects now tended to be spoken of as though it had consisted principally of encouraging a bright and promising group of youngsters to develop an artistic facility of doubtful benefit to their future.

Reasonable enough doubts, however, were expressed as to the wisdom of allowing them to consider art as an easy way to ready money. It was useless quoting the case of Albert Namatjira's financial success, for reports now indicated that the much publicized artists of Central Australia had become a headache to the authorities. True, Albert Namatjira and his more outstanding followers were earning big money. They were big men with their tribe, and they had encouraged a deal of tourist traffic to the 'Red Heart,' but far from encouraging their people to become stable members of the community their success had engendered nothing but irresponsibility. Had they not rich relatives with the wherewithal to provide them with the good things of life, and did not these relatives take the keenest pleasure in indulging their people's every whim?

A new roster was drawn up at Carrolup wherein the boy's leisure time was spent entirely in character-forming pursuits—Scout rallies, organized sport, and 'social activities.' These things were spoken of as innovations, as though the word 'sport' had hitherto been unknown at Carrolup.

An inaugural Scout rally was held amid much enthusiasm and at some expense, but no further meeting was called. A great deal of first-class sporting equipment also arrived at Carrolup about this time in an attempt to wean the boys from an unhealthy enthusiasm for art and from the influence of their teacher outside school hours. This equipment, given out without proper supervision, soon found its way on to the rubbish heap. Still the edict persisted that no art-work was to be carried on after school hours, although nothing was ever organized to replace it.

The superintendent, exhausted and disillusioned after a year's really enthusiastic effort, handed in his resignation about the same time as Mr White received notice of the closing of the school.

Some of the boys were called for by their parents; others, of school-leaving age or near, went off to get whatever jobs were available on farms and in timber-mills. About twenty children with nowhere else to go remained, with nothing to do, until such time as the settlement was reorganized as an agricultural centre.

No one seemed really clear as to how or *why* the school came to be closed or how it was that after such unanimous resolutions the boys were after all dispersed to follow in the footsteps of their people.

Mr White wrote briefly to Mrs Rutter, in London:

> That the education of the boys with whom I was associated has come to an abrupt end is to me a matter of deep personal concern

and regret, but as to the advisability of keeping a school open at Carrolup under the old conditions—that is a Departmental affair. For a while it seemed that there was some vision of what might be achieved for our boys but somewhere, somehow along the road, it became lost.

My wife and I can only hope that the results of our experience will not be wasted and that your efforts in furthering the publicity of our pupil's work may result in better understanding of these unfortunate people and their problems.

Although scattered far and wide the bright, eager faces of our boys smile at us from photographs taken during our happy days at Carrolup. We wonder constantly how they are faring in a not always sympathetic and understanding world and whether any will continue with their art-work on their own initiative. Our good wishes and affection follow them wherever they may be. Although there seems no avenue through which we may again have charge of a group of native children, we continue in the employ of the Educational Department teaching white girls and boys. All teaching is interesting, and it is possible that the results of our work with the children at Carrolup will be more far reaching than we know.

I find that my experience at Carrolup has helped me in my approach towards the artistic development of other children. I have shown my present pupils the Carrolup work, and, using the same methods of motivating them and quickening their observation of nature, now find they are producing art-work well above average standard. Visitors sometimes declare their work is "Carrolup all over again," and it is true that there is something of Carrolup in their work, but those of us who know realize that it is only a shadow of that brilliant, spontaneous creation that came from heaven knows where. Perhaps, however, one or two of these children, may some day *succeed* as artists where those boys of greater talent, lacking other necessary factors, could not.

CHAPTER FOURTEEN

POSTSCRIPT

THOSE who had followed the Carrolup story were interested to read about a year later in *The West Australian* the following newspaper comment:

> The Carrolup Native Settlement, which was closed some time ago for a 'clean-up' and renovations, is now functioning under a new name and with a new training policy. The name is now Marribank Farm School, the object of the Department being to develop the school to provide rural and technical training facilities for young men and boys. . . . The farm covers about 5000 acres, and at present about twenty boys are resident there. It is intended to develop and expand the property as a revenue-making institution. Technical training will be given the boys who show special aptitude.

This is an encouraging step forward, and the good wishes of all interested in the future of these coloured children are with the project, though it is certain that with water-shortage, rabbits, and soil problems it will provide an uphill battle to run as a "revenue-making institution."

A few of the old Carrolup boys are still there and are encouraged to continue with their art-work in leisure hours. The Department is anxious to foster signs of talent or enthusiasm in any field at all and is regretful that its manifestations are so rare. At Moore River Settlement, also in the Great Southern District, a young teacher who worked under Mr White during his last year at Carrolup is being given every opportunity of developing further the teaching experience started there.

"And what," you may ask, "of the other boys, some of whose work is reproduced in this book? Where are they now and what has become of their artistic facility? Are none of them continuing to paint of their own inspiration?"

Some have taken labouring jobs on farms and timber-mills round Katanning and other south-western towns. They are earning good money—some over eleven pounds a week. A few have drifted and appear to be only casually employed. As far as can be ascertained none of the boys are continuing with their art-work. In their leisure time they are drawn to either the local cinemas or the gambling schools that flourish in native camps and on the outskirts of country towns. Their homes are again the squalid camps of their people. Some are contented enough; in others there would seem to rankle a sense of having been some-how let down. Recently one of the brightest and most promising boys, fortified with a quality of 'Dutch courage,' vented his re-sentment against society by hacking a car to pieces with an axe. He was returned to Marribank Farm School as a ward of the state.

It seems hardly likely that any of these boys will achieve much artistically without direction, and for this it may be too late. They feel that they are men now and display no inclination to return either to school or settlement. All their lives as children they had lived for the day when they would be free from the confines of settlements to wander and work as the inclination seized them. For these the stabilizing effect of Mr and Mrs White's influence at Carrolup was interrupted at a crucial time, and all we have now to remind us of their promise are some bright pictures and some exercise-books (now in the possession of the Education Depart-ment) of meticulous neatness and cleanliness, each lesson vividly illustrated.

When questioned now as to their painting the boys seem vaguely troubled. A shadow of bewilderment clouds their dark eyes, as though there was once a vision of beauty, colour, and hope that filled the days with promise and excitement, but the vision faded and was lost.

More than talent is required to make an artist in a modern com-munity. It takes a burning and sustained enthusiasm, and confi-dence, coupled with sufficient measure of self-criticism to stimu-late constant improvement. It requires ambition and staying power besides a *climate* conducive to inspiration and effort such as obviously existed for a while at Carrolup. Besides all this, it requires a place to work and materials to work with.

It has been suggested that a few of the most promising artists should be gathered together again and given some form of direc-tion and encouragement. This may not be impossible, even though the boys show little inclination to be so 'gathered' and suitable accommodation for such a project is not easily obtained.

It is only after the effort of many months that the Department has been able at last to obtain one small house to serve the purpose of a hostel for such promising boys as desire to work in the city or to attend technical colleges.

It can, at least, be hoped that the story of these lost young artists will assist in establishing a firmer educational foundation for all native children, a system in which they may be encouraged to succeed for a definite future and to sustain success into adult life. We may not again see such an artistic flowering as that of the little settlement school, but its unfolding has thrown light into many obscure corners of the past and indicated a way for the future.

The Carrolup children led us to the realization that there can be no such thing as a rubbish-tip of humanity. If man had abandoned these people Nature assuredly had not, for were they not descendants of her closest children—the gentle people of 'dreaming?' They did not know the old songs, the old rites and dances, through which to express their deep and abiding love for and affiliation with a country no longer theirs in name, but with the help of an understanding hand they found a new medium. A garden arose from our rubbish-heap.

What they achieved may not have been aboriginal art, but it was fine old aboriginal love of country—an affirmation of their right to a place in the land of their forefathers. Australia will surely remember these children and those who kindled a lamp for them in a dingy bush schoolroom at a place once called *Carrolup*.

DETAILS OF PAINTINGS

PLATE 1 (*colour*). Pastel.

PLATE 2. Crayon. Very delicate background of mauve shading into pale pink, the design in black.

PLATE 3. Crayon. Deep pink shading up into pale primrose yellow, the leaves and nuts in green and brown.

PLATE 4. Pastel. Deep mauvish pink shading up into pale shell pink, the decorations in natural colours.

PLATE 5. Pastel. Shaded blues, the decorations in brown.

PLATE 6. Crayon. Pink, the decorations in brown.

PLATE 7. Crayon. Deep mauvish pink shading into pale pink, the decorations in natural colours.

PLATE 8. Crayon. A golden-red sunset, reflected on the trees.

PLATE 9. Pastel. Predominating colours blue and yellow.

PLATE 10 (*colour*). French Pastel.

PLATE 11. Water-colour. The trees in natural green, the foreground and sky a glowing yellow.

PLATE 12. Water-colour. The ground in fairly bright greens and yellows against a cloudless golden evening sky, the foliage in black.

PLATE 13. Water-colour. The ground in jade green, a vivid yellow evening light reflected on the trees, the foliage in black.

PLATE 14. Water-colour. Golden pink evening light, the trees in natural colours, the foreground a soft green.

PLATE 15. Crayon. Soft grey and green.

PLATE 16. Crayon. Grey and black, with soft blue rising moon reflected on the water.

PLATE 17. Crayon. Delicate greens, with yellow moon and reflections.

PLATE 18. Crayon. Shaded browns and green in the dying light of the sun.

PLATE 19 (*colour*). Pastel.

PLATE 20. Pastel. Greyish rocks, blue sky, silvery clouds, bright moon reflecting on the water.

PLATE 21. Pastel. Late afternoon. Predominantly blue and yellow, reflected on the water and the path, the trees in natural colours.

PLATE 22. Chalk. Dark background, grey and yellow foliage, with moonlight on the trees and water.

PLATE 23. Pastel. Grey and black.

PLATE 24. Pastel. Blue and orange. (This picture was exhibited at the Pastel Society's Forty-fifth Annual Exhibition in London, in January 1951.)

PLATE 25. French Pastel. A fiery sunset.

PLATE 26. Pastel. Opalescent sky, trees in natural colours reflecting glow from the setting sun.

PLATE 27. Chalk. Moonlight scene in grey and yellow. (The main feature is a blackboy-tree, or grass-tree, which is indigenous to Western Australia, flowers only once in eight years, and is claimed to be one of the oldest known trees.)

PLATE 28 (*colour*). Crayon.

PLATE 29. Crayon. Silvery moon reflected on water from a blue-grey sky, foreground a purplish blue.

PLATE 30. Crayon. Brown and grey. (Note the position of the ponies and the different treatment of the trees.)

PLATE 31. Pastel. A moonlight scene. (Remarkable for its composition, atmosphere, and the animation of the figures.)

PLATE 32. Pastel. Greenish brown landscape, black foliage, the sky a blueish grey, with clouds pink-tipped from the sinking sun.

PLATE 33. Crayon. On a large sheet of ordinary brown paper (43 inches by 30 inches). Blue sky, pink and golden clouds, deep rose sunset, blue river, grey tree-trunks, black foliage, foreground yellowish green, twig-fires with yellow and red flames.

PLATE 34. Crayon. Blue and pale yellow.

PLATE 35. Crayon. Shaded grey and black, with rising sun strongly reflected on the trees. (Composition noteworthy in one so young.)

PLATE 36. Crayon. Grey and black, with silvery moonlit sky. (Remarkable for atmosphere.)

PLATE I THE BLACKBOY-TREE *Parnell Dempster (13 years)*

PLATE 2 GUM-TREE LEAVES AND NUTS *Ross Jones* (13 *years*)

PLATE 3 — A VASE DECORATED WITH GUM-LEAVES AND NUTS — *Unsigned*

PLATE 4 — AN URN DECORATED WITH ABORIGINAL DESIGNS — *A. Ugle (13 years)*

PLATE 5 THE BLUE PLATE *Reynold Hart* (13 *years*)

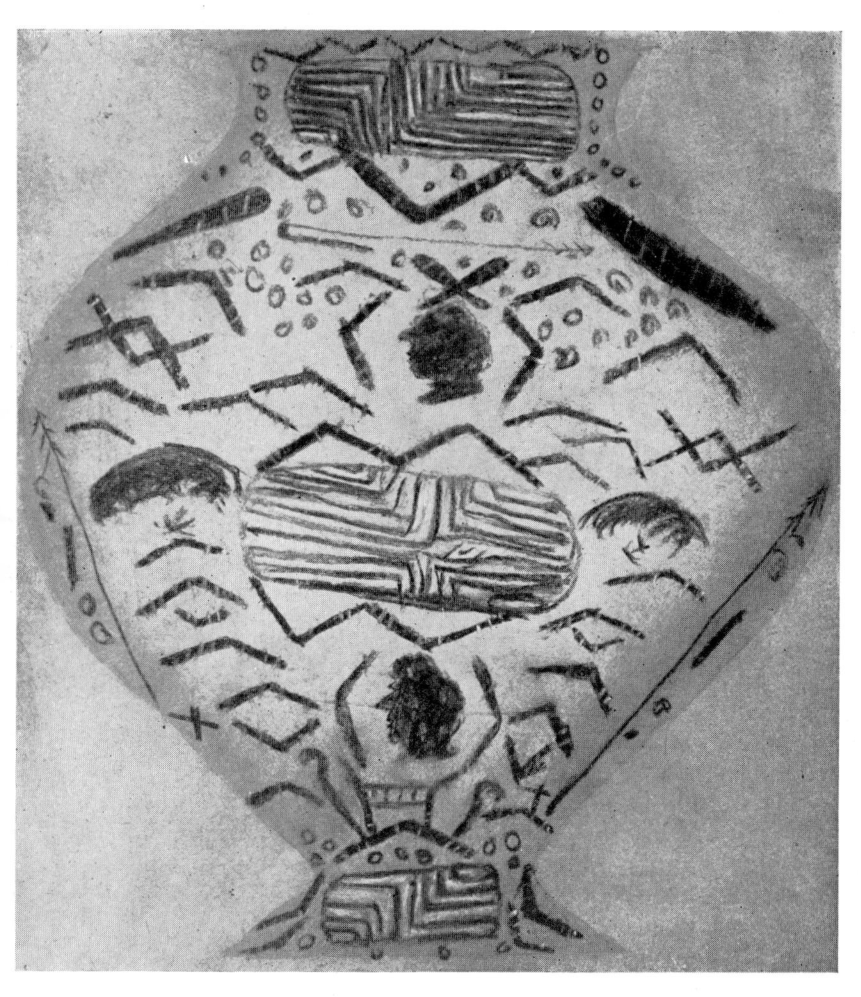

PLATE 6 A VASE DECORATED WITH ABORIGINAL HEADS AND DESIGNS *Unsigned*

PLATE 7 A TEAPOT DECORATED WITH ABORIGINAL DESIGNS *Unsigned*

PLATE 8 THE BLACKBOY-TREE *Parnell Dempster* (13 *years*)

PLATE 9 HUNTING THE 'POSSUM *Unsigned*

PLATE 10 A VIVID SUNSET *Ross Jones (13 ye*

Plate 11 Youth chasing Kangaroo *Reynold Hart* (14 *years*)

PLATE 12 TREES *Revel Cooper (13 years*

PLATE 13 RACING FOR HOME *Revel Cooper* (13 *years*)

PLATE 14 HUNTING *Unsigne*

PLATE 15 PREHISTORIC WOODLAND *Unsigned*

PLATE 16 THE MOONLIT STREAM *Unsigned*

PLATE 17 ALL TRAGIC TO THE MOON *Unsigned*

PLATE 18 THE OLD TREE *Unsigned*

PLATE 19 ON THE ALERT *Barry Loo (13 years)*

PLATE 20 STALKING A SHARK *Claude Kelly* (13 *years*)

PLATE 21 THE FOUR DUCKS *Unsigned*

PLATE 22 GHOST TREES *Unsigned*

PLATE 23 DAWN *Parnell Dempster* (13 *years*)

PLATE 24 DOWN TO DRINK *Parnell Dempster*

PLATE 25 THE BENT TREE *Unsigned*

PLATE 26 CONTENTMENT *Parnell Dempster* (13 *years*)

PLATE 27 TREES IN THE MOONLIGHT *Revel Cooper* (13 *years*)

PLATE 28 — RACING ON THE WING — *Unsigned*

PLATE 29 — THE MOONLIT COAST — *Unsigned*

PLATE 30 WILD PONIES *Cliff Ryder* (13 *years*)

PLATE 31 ON THE LOOKOUT *Barry Loo* (14 *years*)

PLATE 32 KANGAROO AT SUNSET *Parnell Dempster* (13 *years*)

PLATE 33 A NATIVE CORROBOREE *Reynold Hart* (13 *years*)

PLATE 34 HUNTING BY MOONLIGHT *Milton Jackson* (13 *years*)

PLATE 35 THE RISING MOON *Unsigned*

PLATE 36 BENDING TO THE STORM *Parnell Dempster* (12 *years*)